120 Learning Center Activities

Scholastic Inc.

New York • Toronto • London • Auckland • Sydney

Illustrations: David Borchart: 1–14, 27, 41–60, 101–120; Judy Love: 89–92, 93–100;
Chris Reed: 15–26, 28–40, 61–88

Copyright © 1999 by Scholastic Inc.
All rights reserved. Published by Scholastic Inc.
Printed in the U.S.A.
ISBN 0-439-08135-1

1   2   3   4   5   6   7   8   9   10   08   03   02   01   00   99

TABLE OF CONTENTS

Learning Center Activities

![Learning Centers LITERACY CENTER logo]

These activities are easy to set up and are designed for independent use and discovery. Each activity is specifically connected to an **Emergent Reader**. This provides you with a way to observe and assess children's comprehension of concepts in the books. Activities are designed for immediate accessibility: One quick glance will give you the activity's objective, materials needed, even questions for critical thinking to help you in assessment. Each **Emergent Reader** has four connecting cross-curricular activities.

Blocks

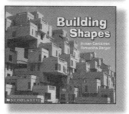

Dramatic Play

Art

Math

Science

Writing

Objective
To explore different kinds of buildings and think about their purposes.

Materials
- blocks
- chart paper
- marker

Critical Thinking
- How could you change a building (like a house) to use it for something else?
- When you look at a building, what clues can you use to discover what it's for?

Guess My Building
How can you tell what a building is for?

1

As a group, brainstorm different kinds of buildings and list them on chart paper.

2

Divide the class into small groups. Each group can choose one kind of building to construct in the block area. Encourage each group to keep the building's purpose to themselves.

3

When children have finished, they can observe and compare the buildings. Let children guess what kind of building each group constructed.

4

Children can then add props (dolls, cars, furniture) to the buildings. Invite children to guess again the kind of building each group constructed. Find out if anyone's guess changed.

supermarket
garage
house

Make a Dream House

Use different materials to make unique houses.

 1

Ask children to imagine their dream house. Encourage them to think about what it would be made of and what it would look like.

 2

Individually or in small groups, children can choose materials and build their dream houses.

 3

Let children decorate their houses with markers or paint.

 4

Then children can describe the houses they've built. Children might want to explain what makes their houses special or why they chose the materials they used.

ART

Objective
To explore how many different kinds of materials can be used for building.

Materials
- rocks, straw, hay, cardboard
- paper (construction paper, shredded paper, newspaper)
- clay
- recycled materials
- glue
- scissors
- markers or paint

Critical Thinking
- How did the materials you chose affect the kind of house you made?

Blocks

Objective

To use a story as a context for considering why certain materials make better houses than others.

Materials

- copy of *The Three Little Pigs*
- paper
- crayons and pencils

Critical Thinking

- Think about houses in other stories. Would it be a mistake to build a house out of gingerbread?
- If there were a fourth little pig, what would he have used?

Blocks

Storybook Houses

What were The Three Little Pigs thinking?

Read *The Three Little Pigs*.

Have a class discussion about the materials the pigs used. Ask children why bricks worked better than hay.

Children can write and draw their own version of the story, substituting other materials for the straw, sticks, and bricks used by the pigs.

Neighborhood Buildings Graph

Take a walk to see what buildings are made of.

 Take children for a walk around your neighborhood. Let them observe the materials buildings are made from and record their findings.

 Back inside, make a graph of the building materials. Use the graph to record how many buildings were made from each material.

 As a class, decide how to count buildings that were made of more than one material.

 Invite children to talk about the buildings they saw and which materials were used most often and least often.

Objective
To make a graph that shows the materials used for buildings in your area.

Materials
- chart paper
- marker
- paper
- pencils
- clipboards

Critical Thinking
- Can you always tell by looking which materials the buildings were made from?
- Why do you think some materials were used more than others?

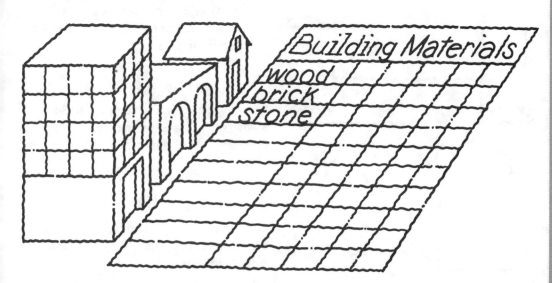

Blocks

Objective

To find out how the shape of a building's base influences the rest of the building.

Materials

- masking tape
- blocks of different sizes and shapes

Critical Thinking

- Does the shape of the base always determine the shape of the building?
- What are some reasons a builder might choose a certain shape for a building?

Build a Shape

Construct buildings from differently shaped bases.

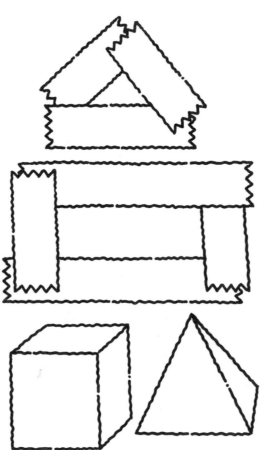

Use masking tape to mark off shapes (circle, triangle, square, rectangle, pentagon) on the floor of the block area.

Help children brainstorm different buildings that would have those shapes. Then invite children to build, using the shapes. They can choose to fill in the base with blocks or just outline it with blocks before building up.

Encourage children to compare buildings made from differently shaped bases. Compare two different buildings with the same base.

As an extra challenge, children can try to make a building whose shape is different from the shape of its base.

Shape City Graph

How many block shapes are used for different buildings?

Objective

To use graphing skills to discover which shapes of blocks are used most often in building.

Materials
- blocks
- large paper for graphing
- marker

Critical Thinking
- Why do you think some block shapes were used more often than others?
- What are other ways to record the kinds of blocks that were used?

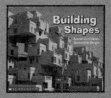

Building Shapes

1

Prepare the graph in advance by drawing shapes across the bottom. Children can also help draw the shapes of different blocks they expect to use in building.

2

Together, make a city. Small groups can each make a different building. Before taking apart the buildings, ask children which kinds of blocks they think they used most often.

3

Take the buildings apart one at a time. Sort the blocks into piles by shape, keeping the piles separate for each building. Talk about which shapes were used most often.

4

Record the building totals of each kind of block in the column for the appropriate shape. Then add up the totals of each shape for all the buildings. Fill in bars to show how many blocks of each shape were used.

SCIENCE

Objective

To create different buildings using the same blocks.

Materials

- blocks of different shapes and sizes

Critical Thinking

- How were the buildings alike and different?
- Would it be a good idea to use only blocks of one shape in a building?

Same Shapes, Different Buildings

What will you build?

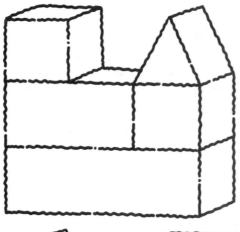

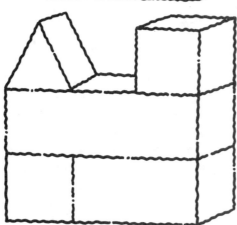

1

Create several sets of blocks that contain the same number of blocks for each shape.

2

Groups of children can use all the blocks in their sets to build any type of building they choose.

3

When they've finished, invite children to examine and compare buildings made by each group. Encourage them to talk about the shapes of the buildings and how the blocks were used to make the different buildings.

Make a Shape Book

Collect shapes to make a class book.

1 Ask children to brainstorm a list of shapes. Count how many different kinds of shapes they can name.

2 Have children search for shapes in magazines, newspapers, and so on. Assign each child a particular shape, or let children find a variety of shapes. Children can cut out the shapes they find.

3 Ask children to glue their shapes onto paper. They can also draw pictures of objects shaped like those on the list.

4 Compile the shape pages into a class book. Write the name of each shape on its page.

Objective

To expand shape vocabulary by finding examples of a large variety of shapes.

Materials

- chart paper
- magazines and newspapers
- scissors
- glue
- drawing paper
- crayons or markers
- stapler

Critical Thinking

- What shapes can you find in the classroom? Can you find more than one of each kind?

Building Shapes

BLOCKS

Objective
To create bridges and explore their uses.

Materials
- blocks of different materials (wood, cardboard), shapes, and sizes
- toys such as cars, trucks, planes, animals, and people

Critical Thinking
- What types of blocks were best for making tall bridges? Wide bridges? Curved bridges?
- Which bridges were best for people to cross? Cars? Trains?

What Will Your Bridge Cross?
Try your hand at building bridges for different purposes.

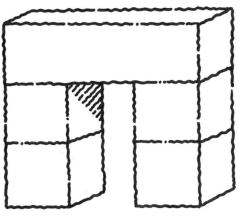

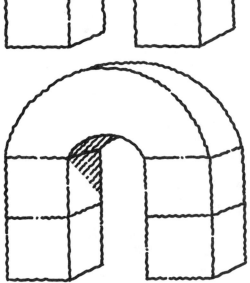

Ask groups of children to build bridges to carry a particular kind of vehicle or to cross a particular place (stream, river, highway, mountain). Encourage children not to tell other groups what kind of bridge they are building.

When finished, children can guess what type of bridge each group built.

When children have finished guessing, have them talk about their bridges. Ask them why they chose the blocks they used. If possible, children can demonstrate how their bridges would be used.

Then have children compare the completed bridges. Children can also use toys to test other groups' bridges.

Test Your Bridge

Experiment with different materials to make bridges.

 1

Have children form pairs or small groups. Place materials in the middle of a table and invite children to choose materials to make a bridge.

 2

When finished, children can test the bridges using small blocks or toys. Then let them find out which bridge can hold the most weight.

 3

After testing, let children change their bridges to make them stronger. They might want to add more materials. Then children can retest the bridges.

 4

Together, compare the bridges. Look for ways the bridges are alike and different.

Objective
To discover which materials make the strongest bridge.

Materials
- assorted materials such as pipe cleaners, paper, cardboard tubes, yarn, clay, straws, rubber bands
- glue
- masking tape
- small blocks or toys
- scissors

Critical Thinking
- Why did some materials work better than others?
- Why is it important to test a bridge before people can cross it?

Bridges

Blocks

Objective

To explore different ways of using the body to make bridges.

Materials

- padded or carpeted floor
- objects to build over, such as large blocks or chairs

Critical Thinking

- Would it be easier to build a bridge with more children or with fewer children? Why do you think so?
- How did the number of children in the group influence the bridges you built?

Bridges

"London Bridge" With a Twist

Use your body to make a bridge.

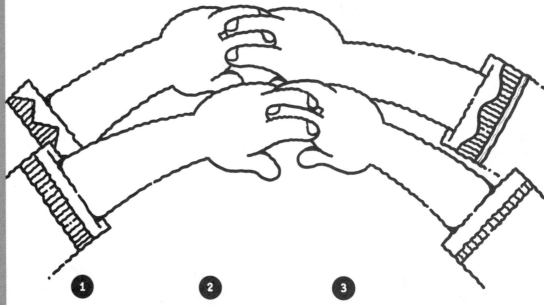

1

Introduce this activity by playing "London Bridge." To play, two children form a bridge by raising their arms and grasping hands. Other children pass under the bridge while singing.

2

Have children form small groups. Give them time to explore how they can use their bodies to make bridges.

3

Challenge the groups to make the longest, lowest, and highest bridges they can. Children can try to build a bridge over a block or a chair.

Let's Make Opposites!
Make a class book of opposite words.

1

Together, discuss words that are opposites. Begin with examples from the book, and follow up by asking children to name other opposite words. Children can also act out opposite words such as *high* and *low*.

2

Introduce the idea of making a class book that shows opposites. Use children's suggestions to make a list of opposites to be included in the book.

3

Let each child choose a friend to work with. Each pair can choose a set of opposites to illustrate.

4

Compile children's opposite drawings into a class book, and enjoy reading it together.

Objective
To expand understanding of opposites.

Materials
- chart paper
- markers
- crayons
- drawing paper
- stapler

Critical Thinking
- Were some pairs of opposites easier to draw than others? Why?
- Can you find examples of opposites in the classroom?

Bridges

Objective

To consider characteristics of different vehicles in designing places for them to park.

Materials

- blocks
- toy vehicles (cars, trucks, trains, buses, airplanes)

Critical Thinking

- How could you build a structure in which two different kinds of vehicles could park?
- What could you add to a garage, train station, or airport to make it a better place for people?

Transportation Station

Build structures in which different kinds of vehicles can park.

 1 Brainstorm a list of vehicles and talk about where they park. Children might want to describe a time they went to the airport, bus station, train station, and so on.

 2 Divide the class into small groups. Let each group choose a kind of vehicle.

 3 Invite children to use the blocks to build a parking structure for their vehicles. Children can decide what the structure will look like and what shape it will have. Ask children how many vehicles it will need spaces for and whether it will need a place for drivers to rest or for travelers to eat.

 4 Encourage children to observe structures built by other groups. Compare structures built for the same kind of vehicles. Children might want to make suggestions for additions to the structures.

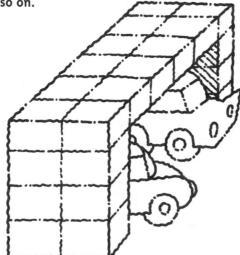

How Do You Park a Kangaroo?

Get silly when thinking about parking different creatures.

Together with children, brainstorm animals that people do and don't ride and where they would "park."

Let each child choose an animal. Children might want to pick animals that people do not normally ride or even make up imaginary animals. Ask children to draw a picture showing how and where they would park their animal.

When finished, children can tell a story about their drawings. They can include where they would ride their animals, what their animals would need, and what the animals' parking spaces would be like.

Bind the pictures together to make a class book. Children's stories can also be included in the book.

Objective
To make a book about how different animals could be "parked."

Materials
- paper
- crayons and markers
- hole punch
- yarn

Critical Thinking
- How is riding an animal similar to and different from driving a car?
- Would it be difficult to use a horse instead of a car or bus to travel around your town?

Blocks

How Many Blocks in a Garage?

Build parking garages for different-sized vehicles.

Objective

To estimate how many blocks it will take to build garages and test these predictions.

Materials

- blocks
- toy vehicles of various sizes (cars, trucks, buses)
- chart paper
- marker

Critical Thinking

- How did the size of the blocks you used affect how many you needed to build the parking structure?

Blocks

 1
Show children toy vehicles of various sizes. Ask children to predict how many blocks they think it will take to build a parking structure for each vehicle. Record their predictions.

 2
Divide the class into small groups, and let each group build a parking structure just the right size for one vehicle. Children might want to build around the vehicle.

 3
When the structures are completed, have each group take apart their building and count how many blocks they used. Compare how many blocks were used with the children's predictions.

 4
Make a graph to show how many blocks it took to build a parking structure for each vehicle.

Make a Transportation Story
Use your imagination to get up and go!

1

Together, talk about favorite trips the children have taken. Ask children to think about where they would go if they could take a trip anywhere.

2

Have children draw pictures to show where they would go on a trip and how they would get there. They can dictate or write stories to go along with the drawings.

3

Hold a special show-and-tell time when children can tell their stories to the class. Encourage children to describe whether they would need to use more than one form of transportation on their trip and if they would see any transportation structures when they arrived.

Objective
To create a story that involves various forms of transportation.

Materials
• markers and crayons
• paper
• pencils

Critical Thinking
• Can you think of more than one way to get to your destination?
• Can you use any kind of vehicle (like a car) to get to any destination (like the moon)?

Blocks

BLOCKS

Objective
To use blocks and props to create a park.

Materials
- chart paper
- paper
- crayons
- blocks
- toy props (people, animals, vehicles)

Critical Thinking
- Did drawing your park before you started building make the park easier to build? Did you make changes to your plan once you started building?
- What is your favorite real park?

Magical Mystery Park

Let your imagination run wild as you create your perfect park!

 Together, talk about parks you have visited. Ask children to imagine their perfect park. Brainstorm things the park might have, and record these ideas on chart paper.

 Have children use crayons and paper to design their ideal park.

 Divide the class into small groups. In the block area, each group can use blocks and props to build their parks.

 When finished, let children compare parks and describe their parks to each other.

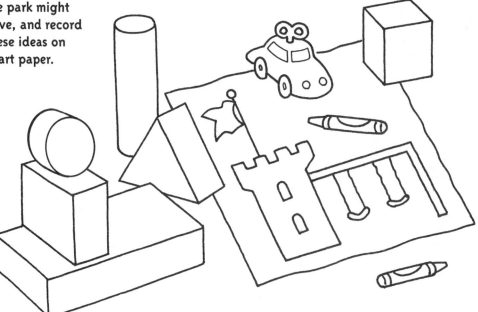

Down the Slide

See how fast things can go down ramps.

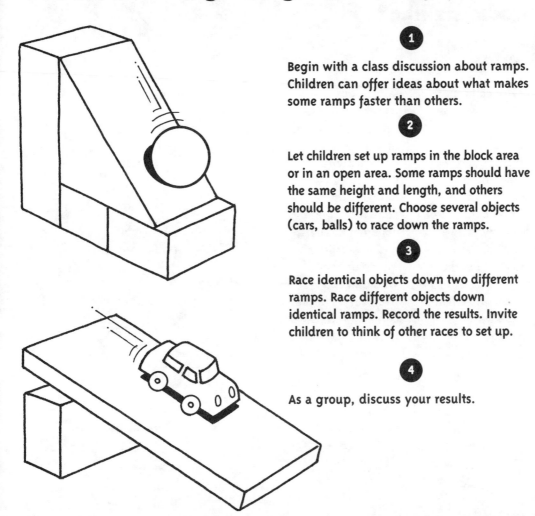

1

Begin with a class discussion about ramps. Children can offer ideas about what makes some ramps faster than others.

2

Let children set up ramps in the block area or in an open area. Some ramps should have the same height and length, and others should be different. Choose several objects (cars, balls) to race down the ramps.

3

Race identical objects down two different ramps. Race different objects down identical ramps. Record the results. Invite children to think of other races to set up.

4

As a group, discuss your results.

Objective

To compare how objects go down ramps with different angles.

Materials

- boards
- blocks
- balls
- toy cars
- chart paper
- markers

Critical Thinking

- Why did some objects go down a ramp faster than others?
- What could you do to make things go down a ramp faster or slower?

Blocks

Objective

To use a variety of materials to design an underwater park.

Materials

- mural paper
- markers and crayons
- paint and brushes
- construction paper
- scissors
- glue
- collage materials

Critical Thinking

- What kinds of things would NOT be possible in an underwater park?

Make an Underwater Playground

What do you think an underwater park would be like?

1

Invite children to imagine what an underwater park would look like. Suggest that they think about whether there would be dry areas and how they would enter and leave the park. Children can also discuss how fish could swim through the park.

2

Spread out mural paper on the floor. Let children design and draw their underwater park. Children can use paint, markers, construction paper, collage materials, and any other art materials they would like. If necessary, children can also form small groups to work on different parts of the park.

3

Hang the mural on the wall for all to enjoy.

Adopt a Park

Take a class trip to help a local park.

1

Take a field trip to a local park. While in the park, discuss ways the park could be improved. Take pictures of places in the park that need improvement, or let children draw pictures to illustrate those places.

2

Back in the classroom, children can write a class letter about the park. Be sure to include captions for the drawings or photos. Children can also draw pictures to show their ideas for improvement.

3

Mail the letter, photos, and drawings to city council members, the mayor, and anyone else who might be able to work to improve the park. Encourage family members to write letters as well.

Objective

To use a trip to a local park to generate ideas for improvement.

Materials

- paper
- pencils or crayons
- clipboards
- camera with film (optional)

Critical Thinking

- What are other things you could do on your own to improve the park?
- Look at parts of the park that need cleaning or repair. How did they get to be that way?

What's in a **Park?**

DRAMATIC PLAY

Objective

To make a nursery in the dramatic-play area.

Materials

- chart paper
- markers
- baby dolls
- baby furniture, props
- cardboard boxes, shoe boxes
- paint and brushes
- water table or plastic tubs

Critical Thinking

- What can parents do if they have to take their babies someplace that is not set up for babies?

A Place for Babies

What goes in a nursery?

 1

Discuss with children what babies need. Let them visit the dramatic-play center to find out whether it contains everything a baby would need. List additional props that would make the center a place for newborns—for example, burp cloths, bottles, pacifiers, booties, and diapers.

 2

Invite children, especially those with new brothers and sisters, to bring in additional props from home. Children can also create props and furniture by painting boxes. Boxes can become strollers, infant seats, bassinets, mobiles, and car seats.

 3

Encourage children to take care of the babies in the dramatic-play center. Remind them to treat newborns gently.

 4

Children can wash the babies in the water table or in plastic tubs. Extend play by moving the activity outdoors on warm days.

Baby Doll Visiting Day

Bring your favorite baby doll to school.

1

Send home a note informing parents about the "Bring a Baby to School" day several days in advance. Before children bring baby dolls or stuffed animals from home, encourage them to think about any changes that the class may need to make to prepare the room for the babies.

2

Begin the day with a special show-and-tell. Invite children to introduce their babies or stuffed animals to the group.

3

Encourage children to keep their babies with them throughout the day. Ask children to consider what they will do with their babies on the playground and during lunch or snacktime, as well as how often their babies will need naps and feedings.

4

At the end of the day, discuss children's experiences with baby care.

Objective
To experience spending an entire day caring for a "baby."

Materials
- baby dolls brought from home
- baby props from dramatic-play center

Critical Thinking
- Did you have to change what you did during the day to accommodate your baby?
- What would your day be like if you had to take care of twins?

Objective

To work as a group to create a baby quilt.

Materials

- squares of different kinds of fabric
- permanent markers
- scissors
- tapestry needles
- yarn

Critical Thinking

- When making something for a baby rather than a grown-up, what are some things that we have to do to make it safe?
- What else could you make that a baby would use?

Make Something for Baby

Decorate your own blanket.

 1

Invite children to choose a fabric square to decorate. Explain that it will become part of a class baby quilt.

 2

Encourage children to decorate their fabric squares very carefully because the markers are permanent. Some children might cut shapes out of different fabric to attach to their square. You may need to help them sew on the pieces.

 3

Help children sew the completed squares together to make a quilt.

4

As a group, decide who should receive the quilt. Some possibilities might include a class member whose family has a new baby or a teacher in the school. Children might also consider donating the quilt to a family shelter.

Comparing Baby and Me

How are babies like you?

1

Have a group meeting to talk about things that five-year-olds (or the age group of your class) need. Ask children whether their needs are the same as or different from a baby's needs. Invite children to make drawings that show things they need.

2

Encourage children to write or dictate stories to accompany their drawings. In their stories, children might want to explain how their needs compare to a baby's needs.

3

Bind the stories together into a class book and invent a title, such as "What Do We Need?" Place the book in the dramatic-play area to be read to the babies there.

Objective

To create a story that compares older children and babies.

Materials

- paper
- crayons and markers
- pencils

Critical Thinking

- Why do babies need different things than older children do? Besides being smaller, how are babies different?
- What do you think your needs will be when you grow up? How will they change?

Objective

To extend dramatic play in the kitchen area beyond cooking.

Materials

- chart paper
- markers
- kitchen props and toy furniture
- assorted boxes
- paint and brushes
- paper
- scissors
- glue
- tin cans (empty)

Critical Thinking

- What activities happen in your home in rooms other than the kitchen?

More Than Cooking

What happens in the kitchen besides cooking?

As a group, make a list of things that people do in the kitchen and be sure to include non-cooking activities. To get started, you might want to ask children to describe what happens after meals.

Invite children to choose activities from the list to act out. Some possibilities might include washing dishes, making a shopping list, putting away groceries, setting the table, and talking about each other's day.

To act out some of the kitchen activities, children might want to create additional props from boxes or other recyclable materials. They can make food labels for boxes or empty cans. Larger boxes can be turned into cabinets, tables, or appliances such as a refrigerator or microwave. Don't forget to bring in a newspaper for reading!

Word Endings

What other words end with -*ing*?

Discuss word endings with children and talk about how they sound. Point out how many words end with -*ing* and what these words have in common.

Invite children to think of other words that end with -*ing*. These words might describe what they do on the playground or when they go shopping. Make a list of the words.

Children can draw pictures to show the -*ing* words from the list. Some children may want to cut out photos from magazines instead. Encourage children to make up a story that includes these words.

Write the words that children illustrate on the pages.

Objective

To explore and make a collection of -ing words (gerunds).

Materials

- chart paper
- paper
- crayons and markers
- magazines
- scissors
- glue

Critical Thinking

- Were some words easier to illustrate than others?
- Can you think of other common word endings?

Dramatic Play

Objective

To illustrate and follow a recipe.

Materials

- chart paper
- crayons and markers
- oven
- muffin tin, liners
- large mixing bowl, 3 smaller bowls
- measuring cups and spoons
- ingredients

Critical Thinking

- Why is it important to measure your ingredients carefully?
- What would happen if you ran out of one of the ingredients?

What's Cooking?

Follow a class recipe to cook up a special treat.

1 Prepare by writing the muffin recipe on chart paper. Have a class discussion about favorite dishes. Ask children whether they have ever followed a recipe to make some of their favorites.

2 Review the muffin recipe. Create a picture chart (rebus) for the recipe. Children can decide how ingredients and quantities should be represented and work together on the drawings.

3 Measure, pour, and mix all of the dry ingredients in the large bowl. Stir in the vanilla, oil, juice concentrate, and banana. Let children fill their muffin liners halfway. Invite them to mix raisins, cinnamon, or peaches into their batter. Cook the muffins at 400° for 20 minutes.

4 Let cool, and eat!

Muffin Ingredients
- 1 cup flour
- 1/2 teaspoon baking powder
- 1/2 teaspoon baking soda
- 1/4 teaspoon vanilla
- 1/4 cup vegetable oil
- 1/4 cup apple juice concentrate
- 1 ripe banana (mashed)
- raisins
- cinnamon
- peaches (optional)

A Cookbook of Our Own

Children describe recipes in their own words.

Objective
To make a class cookbook of favorite (and silly!) recipes.

Materials
- paper
- crayons and markers
- pencils
- stapler

Critical Thinking
- Can you think of some recipes that do not require cooking?
- Can you tell what ingredients are in something just by looking at it?

1

Invite children to think of their favorite recipes. These recipes can be real or made up.

2

Have children write or dictate their recipes. They can use their imagination or describe how they think something is made, even if they aren't certain. Some of these recipes might be pretty silly!

3

When finished, children can draw pictures of what the dish should look like after it's made. They can also add pictures of other foods that they would like to eat along with it.

4

Bind the pages together to make a class cookbook to use in the dramatic-play area.

Dramatic Play

Objective

To plan and act out parties with different themes.

Materials

- dramatic-play props (dishes, costumes, and pretend food)
- construction paper
- scissors
- markers and crayons

Critical Thinking

- Would it be hard to have a party without planning in advance?
- Did you ever discover you had forgotten something after a party started?

It's a Party

Let's Have a Party!

Turn your dramatic-play area into a place for celebration.

1

Encourage children to choose a different kind of party (birthday, pizza, tea, costume) to have in the dramatic-play area each week. Choose one to start with, and brainstorm a list of items needed.

2

Invite children to make decorations and hats for the party and to create additional props that may be needed.

3

Have the party! Children can enact a party at a special time each week, or props can be left out all week for impromptu role-playing.

4

Extend children's experiences by taking a class trip to the library to find out about parties in other cultures.

It's a Writing Party
Make writing fun by preparing for a party!

1

As a group, brainstorm different types of parties you could have at school. Suggestions might include a Hat Party, Teddy Bear Tea, Backward Party, or Pajama Party. Write the suggestions on chart paper, and vote on one kind of party to host.

2

Encourage children to think about the party's date, time, location, and how people will RSVP. Ask them to make invitations with this information.

3

Send out the invitations to parents, caregivers, or other classes. Before the party date, let children make lists of what is needed for the party. Some children might want to create banners for the room. Others can make signs to direct guests to the party.

4

Finish party preparations, and enjoy the party!

Objective
To practice writing skills by creating invitations, to-do lists, and signs.

Materials
- chart paper
- markers and crayons
- paper
- envelopes

Critical Thinking
- How does writing a list help you get ready for a party?
- How could we add to our signs so that children who have not yet learned to read can find the party?

Party is here

You're Invited

Party to do list
get cake
decorate
send invitations

It's a Party

Dramatic Play

COOKING

Objective

To use math skills while preparing a party snack.

Materials

- 1/2 watermelon
- cantaloupe, honeydew, apples, grapes, strawberries
- lemon
- knife
- melon baller (or spoon)
- measuring cups
- granola

Critical Thinking

- What would you do if one of your guests was allergic to the food you were serving?

It's a Party

Dramatic Play

A Watermelon Feast

What's a party without food?

1 As a group, make a list of fruits that might go into a fruit salad. Invite children to help prepare a fruit salad inside a watermelon!

2 Children can use a melon baller (or metal spoon) to hollow out the watermelon. They can also make melon balls from cantaloupe and honeydew melons. Other children can help cut up apples or strawberries or pull grapes off their stems.

3 While preparing the fruit, children can count the pieces of each kind of fruit and use a measuring cup to measure an equal amount of each type of fruit.

4 Place the fruit back in the watermelon shell and squeeze lemon juice on top. Sprinkle granola on top immediately before serving. Enjoy!

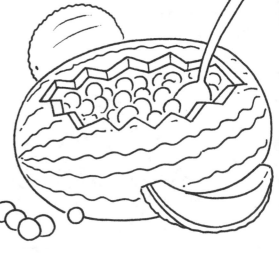

Decorate a Jungle

Transform your classroom to create an unusual party atmosphere.

1

Tell children that they are going to take a pretend visit to the jungle to have a party. If possible, visit the library for books about the jungle.

2

Divide the class into small groups, and ask each group to be responsible for a different part of the room. Children can think about what plants and animals they might find in the jungle, what the weather might be like, and what food they would serve.

3

Let children use art materials to decorate the room so that it looks like a jungle. They can add to their work over a few days to make the transformation complete.

4

Have a party in your new room, and invite other classes in for a peek! You might even want to add jungle food and costumes.

Objective
To learn about the jungle environment by decorating the classroom.

Materials
- butcher paper
- construction paper
- scissors
- glue
- paint and brushes
- markers
- crayons

Critical Thinking
- What other kinds of places can we turn our room into?
- If you could go to a party in any part of the world, where would it be? Why?

It's a Party

Dramatic Play

Objective

To explore children's experiences and feelings about what happens in a doctor's office.

Materials

- chart paper
- marker
- medical props (adhesive bandages, gauze, stethoscope, white coat, elastic bandages)
- paper
- crayons
- pencils

Critical Thinking

- How is going to the doctor for a checkup different from going to the doctor when you are sick or hurt?

Going to the Doctor

What happens when you visit the doctor's office?

Brainstorm a list of things that you need to turn the dramatic-play area into a doctor's office. If possible, visit the school nurse's office for first aid ideas and props.

Set up the office and encourage children to play different roles, such as doctor, child, nurse, or parent. Children can also give first aid to dolls or stuffed animals and use paper to write prescriptions.

Invite children to role-play different scenarios. Some might want to act out what happens when they go to the doctor with a sore throat or a stomachache. Others might pretend to go for a checkup.

Children can also talk about any fears they may have about going to the doctor. Play-acting is one of the best ways to deal with these fears.

First Aid Stories

When did you need first aid?

1

Invite children to think about a time they needed first aid or an instance when they might need first aid. As a class, discuss the situations and appropriate treatments.

2

Ask children to write or dictate something that happened to them or to make up a first aid story. On another page, children can describe what they did (or what they would do) for it.

3

Let children illustrate their pages.

4

Bind the pages together to make a class book, and place it in the dramatic-play area to be used as a prop. Doctors or nurses can use it as a "reference," or parents can read it to sick baby dolls.

First Aid Class Book

Objective

To make a class first aid book based on children's experiences.

Materials
- paper
- markers and crayons
- pencils

Critical Thinking
- How can we make our classroom safer?
- If a friend is sick or hurt, how can we help her get better?

Objective

To create bandage designs and use them on paper doll self-portraits.

Materials

- construction paper
- crayons and markers
- tape
- butcher paper
- collage materials
- scissors
- glue

Critical Thinking

- Are there some cuts or scrapes that need more than an adhesive bandage?
- How do such bandages help cuts and scrapes to heal?

Design a Bandage
Laughter is the best medicine!

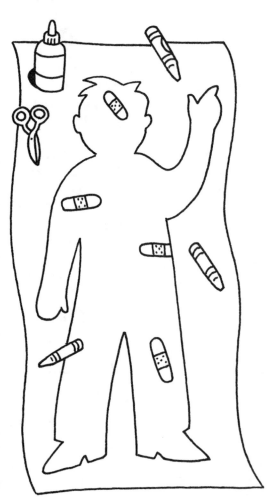

Prepare this activity by cutting out adhesive bandage shapes from construction paper. Ask children to describe the funniest decorations on bandages they've ever seen. Challenge them to make one that's even sillier! Children can use art materials to decorate as many bandages as they want.

Invite children to make body tracings of each other on butcher paper. After cutting out the body shapes, let children tape or glue on the bandages they made.

Encourage children to tell stories about why they needed those bandages.

Children may want to use crayons or collage materials to add to the body tracing details that give clues to the reasons for the bandages!

First Aid Graph

Have you ever needed first aid for any of these things?

1

Invite children to help you make a list of things they have needed first aid for. The list could include scraped knees and elbows, stomachaches, and bruises.

2

Prepare a graph by placing the injuries and illnesses from the list across the bottom or side of chart paper. Children can help illustrate the list.

3

Count how many children have needed first aid for each item on the graph, and put this information in the graph.

4

Use the graph to find out which injuries were the most common and which were the least common.

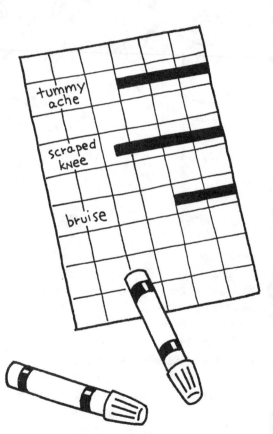

tummy ache

scraped knee

bruise

Objective
To use math skills by graphing incidents when children needed first aid.

Materials
- chart paper
- markers

Critical Thinking
- Could some of the things (injuries, illnesses) on the graph have been prevented? How?
- Do some kinds of injuries need the same first aid treatment?

Dramatic Play

DRAMATIC PLAY

Objective

To role-play how veterinarians take care of animals.

Materials

- stuffed animals
- props such as bandages, pet brushes and combs, toy thermometers
- paper
- pencils
- cardboard boxes
- paint and brushes

Critical Thinking

- What kinds of pets do people have besides cats and dogs? What do these pets need that is different from cats and dogs?

Taking Care of Animals

Turn your classroom into a veterinarian's office.

1

Brainstorm as a group what happens when you take a pet to the vet. Children with pets at home can tell about their experiences with veterinarians.

2

Create a vet's office in the dramatic-play center. Paint boxes to make additional props such as kennels or beds, flea bath, animal scale, and even an X-ray machine!

3

Children can take turns playing the vet and the pet owner. Let children act out different scenarios, such as a puppy being taken for shots, a bird needing a broken wing fixed, or a cat getting washed and groomed.

4

If interested, children might also want to create a pet store. Then they can "buy" a pet and take it to the vet for a checkup!

Meet the Vet

What kinds of animals do vets take care of?

1

Invite a veterinarian to visit the class, or take a field trip to a vet's office. Before the visit, make a list of questions to ask the vet. Children might want to know how she became a vet and what kinds of animals she takes care of.

2

Interview the veterinarian about his job. Find out what kinds of things he uses to treat animals or what was the most unusual animal he ever treated.

3

After the visit, children can make thank-you cards to send to the vet by drawing or writing about what they learned. Children might also want to make changes to the dramatic-play area based on what they learned.

4

Encourage children to use their new knowledge in role-playing.

Objective
To find out about the work veterinarians do.

Materials
- chart paper
- paper
- crayons and markers
- pencils
- clipboards

Critical Thinking
- What do vets do that is similar to what doctors do? What is different?
- Would a vet working in the country take care of different pets than a vet working in a city?

Dramatic Play

Objective

To dream up and create an imaginary pet.

Materials
- paper
- crayons and markers
- pencils

Critical Thinking
- What kind of pet would you have if you lived in a really small home? What if you lived on a farm?
- What kinds of things would your imaginary pet need if it came to life?

Dramatic Play

Invent a Pet

How silly can you get when you create a pet?

Invite children to dream up an imaginary pet. Ask them to think about what it would look like and where it would live.

Children can use crayons and markers to draw their pets.

Encourage children to make up a story about their imaginary pets. Children can describe what the pets would do while the children are at school or on the weekends. Children can write or dictate their stories. Some children might want to draw additional illustrations.

Put the stories together to make a class book the children can enjoy.

Animal Observation

"Adopt" a pet to learn about animals.

1

Divide the class into small groups. Invite each group to "adopt" a pet by choosing an animal to observe. This animal could be a classroom pet, a bug found on a plant, or an animal that can be observed outdoors, such as a squirrel.

2

Encourage children to observe their pet animal every day during the course of a week. Remind them to keep track of their observations by writing or drawing what they see. Children can also record what they hear, feel, or smell.

3

At the end of the week, members of each group can make a presentation to report what they discovered about the animal they observed.

My Animal Chart

Objective

To observe an animal carefully and record it. behavior.

Materials

- paper
- pencils
- crayons and markers

Critical Thinking

- How are animals that live outdoors different from pets that can live indoors?
- Did the animal you observed do anything that surprised you?

Pet Care

Dramatic Play

Objective

To explore painting with a wide variety of objects.

Materials

- paint
- paper
- foam brushes
- feathers, yarn, leaves, pine needles, corncobs, corn husks, roll-on bottles, squirt bottles, squeeze bottles

Critical Thinking

- Were some tools easier to use for painting than others? Can you think of other unusual objects you could paint with?

Painting Tools

Create with more than just brushes.

 Place a variety of painting tools on a table. Invite children to choose one to paint with. They might want to paint with their paper on the table, an easel, or even on the floor.

 Encourage children to try painting the same shape or using the same color with a variety of tools. Children can compare and contrast paintings made with different tools.

 Some children might want to try painting something specific, such as an animal, a house, or a person. Ask them to choose the tool they think would be best for what they plan to paint.

4 Display the paintings on a wall or spread them out on a table. Challenge children to match the painting to the tool used to make it.

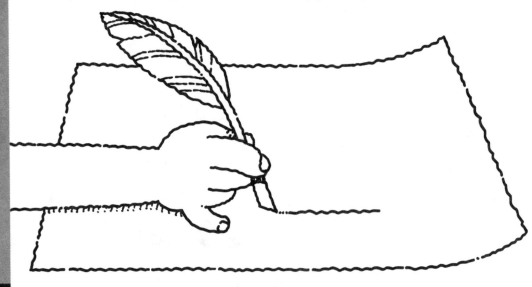

Painting Surfaces

What can you paint on besides paper?

1 Spread various types of paper on the table. Invite children to touch and compare the various surfaces. Encourage them to predict which will work best for painting. Children can test their predictions.

2 After exploring one type of paint, children can try different kinds of paint on one type of paper at a time.

3 Expand your experiment to include non-paper surfaces, and compare the results.

4 To extend the activity, experiment with mixing materials into paint and observing how surfaces react to the modified paint. You could try mixing paint with shaving cream, sand, baby oil, flour, salt, soap, or glue.

SCIENCE

Objective
To find out how different surfaces and materials react to paint.

Materials
- paint (tempera, watercolor, fingerpaint)
- paintbrushes
- paper (fingerpaint, textured, wrapping, construction)
- other painting surfaces (wood, cardboard, rocks, foil)

Critical Thinking
- Why do you think some kinds of paper hold paint better than others?

WHAT DO ARTISTS USE?

Art

Objective

To decorate shoe boxes as cars and build a parade route.

Materials

- shoe boxes
- paint
- paintbrushes
- glue
- scissors
- construction paper and other collage materials
- blocks

Critical Thinking

- How did the size and number of cars affect the parade route?
- What other parade themes could you have?

Art Car Parade

Have you ever seen a shark car?

 As a group, discuss parades that the children have seen. Ask children about what they saw in the parades and what the parades were for.

 Invite children to each decorate a shoe box as a car that will be in a class parade. Some children might want to transform their shoe box into something specific, such as an animal or a hat. Others might want to decorate their box with feathers, sparkles, yarn, even wings or rubber spiders!

 Build a parade route in the block area. Have children consider the cars that will be in the parade, the parade route, and places for spectators. They also might want to build bridges or tunnels for the cars.

 Line up the cars and have a parade!

"Me" Poster

Make a poster that shows what you're really like.

1

As a group, discuss self-portraits. Ask children what they show about the person represented. Find out if children have other ideas about how they could show something about themselves without drawing a self-portrait.

2

Invite children to create a poster that gives clues about what they are really like. Children might want to include pictures of things they like or souvenirs from places they have visited. They can also include objects that remind them of things they have done or of special people.

3

Some children might want to bring items from home to include in their posters.

4

Set up a display of the posters for children to observe. Children can guess who created which poster. Let children explain their posters and why they included the items they did.

Objective

To use media creatively to make an alternative self-portrait.

Materials
- posterboard
- paint and brushes
- glue
- scissors
- collage materials
- construction paper
- magazines and newspapers

Critical Thinking
- Did you find out something new about your friends from their posters?
- What other ways could you show somebody what you are really like?

Art

Objective
To explore styles used by well-known artists.

Materials
- art books or reproductions of paintings
- paper
- paint
- paintbrushes

Critical Thinking
- Were some kinds of paintings more difficult to describe than others? Why?
- When you look at a painting, what are some clues about how long ago it was painted?

Discover Artists

Try out the techniques of different artists.

1 Find reproductions (prints, posters, art books) of work by artists with fairly distinctive styles. Possible artists include Picasso, Monet, and Jackson Pollack. Children might also enjoy the work of collage artists.

2 As a class, observe and compare the work of various artists. Encourage children to notice how these artists use shapes and colors, and ask them to describe what they see in the paintings.

3 Invite children to each choose an artist and experiment with the style of that artist. Ask them to use their own ideas instead of trying to copy a painting they have seen. Some children might want to try using materials other than paint.

4 Have a class show-and-tell when children can describe their paintings.

Museum Art

Use a museum visit as inspiration for a classroom gallery.

1

Visit a museum to see how art is displayed. Encourage children to find different kinds of paintings, such as landscapes, still lifes, and portraits. Draw children's attention to elements outside of the paintings themselves, including frames, titles, and labels.

2

Help children set up an art museum in the classroom. Let children choose the type of painting they would like to make.

3

When finished, invite children to title their paintings and write or dictate a label explaining them. Children can also decorate cardboard or posterboard for a frame.

4

As a class, decide how to display the paintings in the room, and invite other classes to visit your museum. You may want to divide your gallery into different sections for still lifes, portraits, landscapes, and other types of paintings.

Objective
To find out about different kinds of paintings and how they can be displayed.

Materials
- paper
- paint
- paintbrushes
- cardboard or posterboard
- pencils
- index cards

Critical Thinking
- How can you use a painting to tell a story?
- How is a painting different from a photograph?

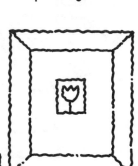

In a Painting

SCHOLASTIC

Art

Objective

To discover how colors combine to make new colors.

Materials

- paper
- powdered tempera paint (red, yellow, blue)
- ice cubes

Critical Thinking

- What happens if we add more of one color than another?
- Would the paintings turn out differently if we used more or less ice?

Ice Painting

Find out about mixing colors the "cool" way.

1

Sprinkle two colors of tempera paint onto each child's paper, keeping the two colors separate.

2

Give children ice cubes and encourage them to rub the ice on the paint. Observe what happens to the ice cube and to the colors on the paper.

3

Explore different combinations of colors. Some children might want to add more paint powder to paper they are already working on.

Color Graphs

What's your favorite color?

1

As a group, ask children to name their favorite colors. Make a list that shows who likes each color.

2

Make a graph of "Our Favorite Colors," listing the colors across the bottom. Ask children whether some colors were much more popular than others or whether choices were spread fairly evenly among different colors.

3

Encourage children to use unit blocks to make other color graphs. Some possibilities include graphing the colors found in the classroom or in a favorite book (how many brown, blue, yellow objects appear in the book).

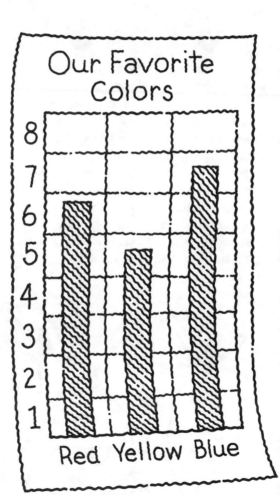

Our Favorite Colors

Red Yellow Blue

MATH

Objective

To use math skills in making different kinds of graphs.

Materials

- chart paper
- markers
- unit blocks
- picture books

Critical Thinking

- Would it matter whether we listed the colors along the side of the graph instead of across the bottom?
- How would we have to change the graph to include another class's favorite colors?

In a Painting

Art

Objective

To explore the insides of apples while making prints with them.

Materials

- apples
- knife
- sponge cloth
- paint
- paper

Critical Thinking

- Did using different amounts of paint affect how the prints turned out?
- What do you think prints would look like if you used a juicier fruit, like an orange or a lemon?

Apple Prints

Have you ever painted with an apple?

1 Begin by cutting some apples vertically and others horizontally. Apples can also be cut at varying distances from the ends. Pass around the cross-sections so that children can observe the insides. Ask if they can find the star in the middle.

2 Pour paint onto a sponge cloth to make a "stamp pad." (If no sponge cloth is available, pouring a little paint onto a paper plate works well.) Each child can choose a cross-section to make prints with.

3 Encourage children to try different apple cross-sections and different colors and amounts of paint. Some children might want to make a pattern on their prints.

4 Rinse the apples to remove the paint and compare the apples to the prints. Try to match the prints to the apples used to make them.

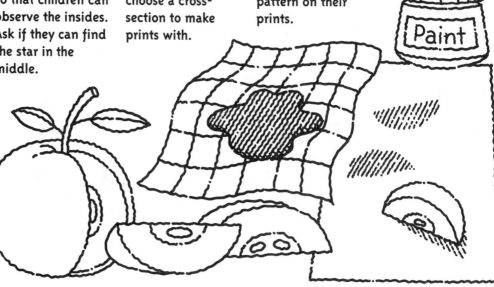

Comparing Apples

They're different, but they're all the same fruit.

①

Prepare this activity by gathering and cutting up a variety of apples. Place one type of apple on each plate, and keep a whole apple next to the plate for comparison. A clipboard can be placed next to each plate for children to record their observations.

②

Invite children to taste and compare the different apples. Encourage them to record their observations with words and/or drawings.

③

Try to sort the apples. Children may want to group them based on color, size, or flavor.

④

Just for fun, do a "blind" taste test. When blindfolded, children can compare two different kinds of apples or try to guess which kind of apple they are tasting.

Objective

To compare and contrast different kinds of apples.

Materials

- apples that vary in size, color, and type
- knife
- plates
- paper
- pencils or crayons
- clipboards

Critical Thinking

- What kind of apple do you think tastes best?
- Do apples taste different when you are blindfolded than they do when you can see them?

apples

Art

MATH

Objective

To create counting books using both collage and drawing.

Materials

- paper
- crayons and markers
- magazines
- scissors
- glue

Critical Thinking

- Are some kinds of objects harder to count than others?
- How would you make a counting book that goes up to 100?

Art

A Combination Counting Book

So many things to count!

 1

Invite children to make counting books of their own. Let children each choose a category of things to include in their book. Some possibilities are fruits, shapes, animals, and cars. Children can also work in small groups, with each child creating a different numbered page.

 2

Children can search magazines for pictures for their books. They can also use crayons or markers to draw objects. Encourage children to use a combination of magazine pictures and hand-drawn pictures for their counting books.

 3

Finish the books by writing the numeral form and name of each number on its page.

 4

For variation, children might want to make books that count by twos or threes. Collage materials (feathers, felt pieces, pompoms) could also be used instead of pictures.

Apple Snack

What can you make with apples?

 1

Help children cut up the apples. Stir lemon juice with the apples in the baking dish.

 2

Mix oats, flour, and cinnamon in the bowl. Let children help measure ingredients and stir. Add just enough oil to make dough crumbly. Sprinkle this mixture over the apples.

 3

Broil for three to four minutes, about 6 inches from the heat.

 4

Let cool, and eat.

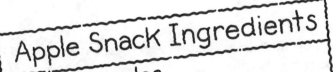

Apple Snack Ingredients

- 2 cups apples
- 2 tablespoons lemon juice
- 6 tablespoons rolled oats
- 4 tablespoons flour
- 1/2 teaspoon cinnamon
- vegetable oil for mixing

Objective

To cook and taste an apple recipe.

Materials
- plastic knives
- measuring cups and spoons
- mixing bowl
- oven-proof baking dish
- oven
- ingredients

Critical Thinking
- How did the apple snack change after you broiled it? Did it look different?
- What would happen if you cooked the apples too long or not long enough?

Art

Objective

To combine a variety of materials to make an animal sculpture.

Materials

- recycled materials (cardboard tubes, boxes, egg cartons)
- nature materials (leaves, bark, twigs)
- paint
- paintbrushes
- glue
- scissors
- collage materials (fabric, feathers, felt, tissue paper)

Critical Thinking

- Did the materials you chose affect what animal you made?

Make Your Own Animal Sculpture

Use recycled materials as inspiration for sculpting.

Place materials on the table. Invite children to choose a variety of materials to make an animal sculpture. Some children might want to work in pairs or small groups to create a larger animal.

Animals can be real, make-believe, or a combination of animals (horse-snake, monster-dragon, elephant-snail).

After putting the sculpture together, children can add finishing touches with glue and collage materials.

Invite children to tell the class a story about their animals and why they decided to make the animals they did.

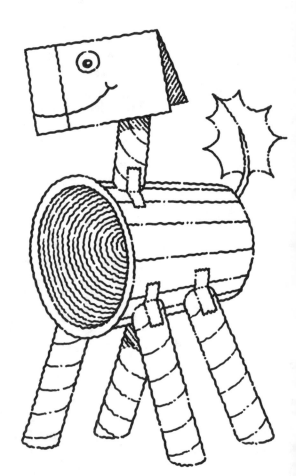

Pretzel Animals

Have you ever heard of edible art?

1

Make pretzel dough together. Measure warm water into mixing bowl. Sprinkle on yeast and stir until soft. Add salt, sugar, and flour. Mix and knead dough.

2

Give children a small ball of dough each, and invite them to make any animal they choose.

3

Grease cookie sheets. Lay sculptures on cookie sheets. Brush pretzels with beaten egg and sprinkle with coarse salt.

4

Bake at 425° for 12 to 15 minutes. Enjoy!

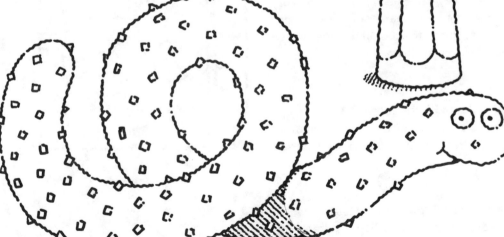

Objective
To mold animal sculptures out of pretzel dough.

Materials
- 1 package yeast
- 1 1/2 cups warm water
- 1 tsp salt
- 1 tbs sugar
- 4 cups flour
- 1 egg, beaten
- coarse salt
- large mixing bowl, spoon, cookie sheets

Critical Thinking
- How did the dough change when we baked it?
- What other foods could you use to make a sculpture?

Objective

To construct a zoo and create animals to live in it.

Materials

- blocks
- toy animals
- construction paper
- scissors
- glue
- markers, crayons
- recycled materials

Critical Thinking

- Why do different kinds of animals need different kinds of environments at the zoo?
- How could you build a zoo section for more than one type of animal?

Build a Zoo

Who lives in the zoo?

As a group, talk about the zoo. Ask children to describe different kinds of areas where animals live in the zoo. These sections might include reptile houses, bird cages, fish aquariums, lion cages, monkey houses, and areas for giraffes and elephants.

Invite children to make a zoo out of blocks. They can consider what kinds of animals and how many of each kind they want to put in the zoo, and make sure to build places for them.

Let children fill the zoo with toy animals from the classroom. Children might also like to create animals out of art materials.

Over the next few days, encourage children to create additional animals for their zoo. They might even want to invite parents or friends for a zoo "field trip."

Animal Story

What would happen if the toy animals in our class came to life?

 1

Gather toy animals from the classroom. Children can also bring stuffed animals from home.

 2

As a group, make up an add-on story about what would happen if the toy animals came to life. Invite children to think of adventures that the animals could have, both inside and outside the classroom. Have one child begin the story and other children each add a sentence or two.

3

Write each child's section on a separate sheet of chart paper.

4

Let children use crayons or markers to illustrate the story. Read it together as a big book.

Objective

To create a fantasy animal story as a class

Materials

• chart paper
• paper
• crayons and markers
• toy animals

Critical Thinking

• Would it matter whether the animals in the story stayed the same size as the toys or became their real size?

• What do real animals need to live in the wild?

Art

Objective

To explore clay by making sculptures.

Materials

- clay or play dough
- modeling tools (cookie cutters, plastic knives, craft sticks)
- materials for impressions (cardboard, beads, sandpaper)
- decorations (pipe cleaners, leaves, twigs, buttons)

Critical Thinking

- How did the color of the clay affect what you made with it?

Clay Creations

Create wacky clay sculptures and more.

1

Invite children to make a clay sculpture. Begin by working with the clay with hands only. Ask children to note the texture, temperature, and color of the clay.

2

Let children choose a tool to work with. Encourage them to find out what they can do with the tools—what kinds of shapes they can make or how they can change the form of the clay. Compare different tools.

3

Provide materials for making impressions in the clay. Children can find out which objects or materials make the clearest impression and whether some are easier to work with than others.

4

Ask children to choose materials to decorate their clay creations. Some children might want to choose a variety of materials, and others might want to work with only one kind of decoration.

Searching for Clay

Go on a "clay" treasure hunt.

1

Begin by asking children to name objects they have seen that are made from clay. Make a list of these objects.

2

Take clipboards and go on a "treasure hunt" for clay objects. (If few clay objects are found, a material like cement could be substituted.) You could begin your search in the classroom, expand it to the school, and then into the neighborhood. Write down all the clay objects that you see.

3

Make a graph of the objects from your lists. Ask children what kinds of objects were found most often.

4

As an extension, children can search for clay objects in their homes. Add this information to your graph.

Objective

To find clay objects and make a graph representing them.

Materials

- objects made of clay
- paper
- pencils
- clipboards
- chart paper

Critical Thinking

- Can you think of anything else the objects you found could be made of?
- What do the objects made from clay have in common?

Art

Objective

To cook play dough, observe the changes, and use it for sculpting

Materials

- measuring cups and spoons
- saucepan, stove
- airtight container
- 4 cups flour
- 4 cups water
- 2 cups salt
- 8 teaspoons cream of tartar
- 2 tablespoons oil
- food coloring

Critical Thinking

- What happens when you mix together two colors of play dough?

Art

Do-It-Yourself Play Dough

Play dough is more fun when you cook it yourself.

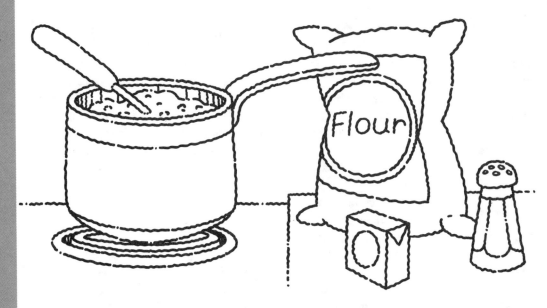

1 Combine ingredients in a saucepan. Invite children to help measure, pour, and stir.

2 Cook over low heat, stirring constantly until mixture thickens and forms a dough. Cool, knead, and store in an airtight container.

3 You might want to mix in materials to add texture. Possibilities include rice, sand, glitter, and oats.

4 After sculpting, play dough can also be baked to harden it.

Clay Props

What do you need for your dramatic-play area?

1

As a group, visit the dramatic-play center. Ask children to think about what could be added to improve the center. Some objects could be for decoration only. Make a list of their suggestions.

2

Invite children to choose objects from the list to make from clay. Some children might want to make kitchen items such as bowls or plates, and others might want to make something for decoration like a sculpture or a plaque.

3

Encourage children to decorate their objects. Fabric or pipe cleaners could be added while the clay is still soft. After the objects dry, children can paint them or glue on materials like sequins, foil, or fabric.

4

Add the finished products to your dramatic-play area.

Objective

To make clay objects to add to the dramatic-play area.

Materials

- chart paper
- marker
- clay
- modeling tools
- paint and brushes
- decorative materials

Critical Thinking

- Is it easier to decorate your clay props before or after they dry?
- Is there anything you could make that would use clay and some other material, such as cardboard?

Art

Objective

To identify numbers outside the classroom.

Materials

- paper
- pencils
- clipboards
- chart paper
- markers

Critical Thinking

- What is another way you could keep track of the numbers you saw?
- Why do you think we found some numbers more often than others?

NUMBERS
ALL AROUND

Number Hunt

Take a walk to search for numbers.

 1

Prepare for the walk by making tally sheets of numbers. Help children write the numbers 0-9 across the top of their papers, leaving the column below each one empty.

 2

Take a walk through the school and neighborhood to hunt for numbers. Encourage children to keep track of each number they see by making a mark in the appropriate column on their tally sheets. Some children may prefer to work on this activity in pairs or small groups.

 3

After returning to the classroom, make a graph of the numbers you found during the walk. Write the numbers across the bottom of chart paper. Draw a bar above each number to represent how many times it was spotted.

 4

Invite children to talk about the different places they found numbers and which numbers were the most common.

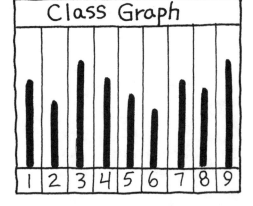

Class Graph

1 2 3 4 5 6 7 8 9

Parking Match

Match the numbers to find a parking space.

 1

Gather toy cars in the block area and count them. Write numbers on paper and tape one to each car.

 2

Invite children to build a garage for the cars out of blocks. Make sure there is one space for every car and mark the spaces with numbers.

3

Ask children to park each car in the matching numbered parking space.

 4

As a challenge, have children perform an arithmetic operation on the car's number in order to find its parking space. For example, children might have to add 2 or subtract 1 from the car's number and park it in the space corresponding to the result.

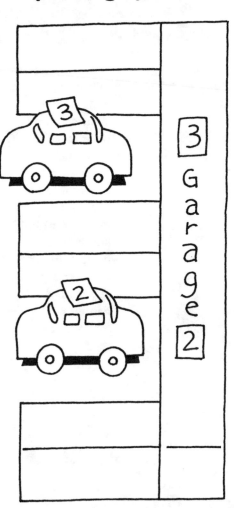

BLOCKS

Objective
To enhance number recognition through a matching game.

Materials
- blocks
- toy cars
- construction paper
- markers
- tape
- scissors

Critical Thinking
- What else could you match using numbers?
- What are other ways you could use numbers in the block area?

NUMBERS
ALL AROUND

Math

Objective

To practice number recognition and writing by incorporating numbers into pictures.

Materials

- paper
- markers and crayons
- collage materials
- scissors
- glue

Critical Thinking

- What are some other ways you can hide a number?
- Where might you hide a number in the classroom?

NUMBERS
ALL AROUND

Hidden Numbers

How can you hide a number?

1

Introduce this activity by talking about hiding. You might want to play hide-and-seek on the playground or look at a *Where's Waldo?* book.

2

Invite children to hide a number in a picture. Some children might want to do this by camouflaging the number so that it blends into the background. Others might want to hide a number so it peeks through part of the foreground (by hiding it behind tree leaves, for instance).

3

Children can also try hiding more than one number, using a combination of art materials. They might want to draw a picture to camouflage some numbers and hide others behind flaps made of collage materials.

4

Challenge children to hide the numbers o through 9 in a picture. When they have finished, children can exchange pictures and try to find the numbers in other children's artwork!

"My Day" Counting Book
We use numbers all day long.

Brainstorm daily activites involving numbers. You might get children started by bringing up activities such as breakfast and bath time.

Give each child nine sheets of drawing paper to make a counting book. Let children illustrate the numbers 1 through 9 with activities they perform daily—for example, a child might get out of 1 bed, put on 2 socks, eat 3 pieces of toast, and so on.

If children have difficulty thinking of ways to illustrate some numbers, they can use their imagination. For example, a child could draw 5 sandwiches or 8 swings, even if he wouldn't really eat 5 sandwiches or swing on 8 swings.

Staple the pages together and put the books in the reading center!

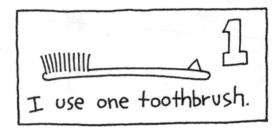

I use one toothbrush.

I wear two socks.

I eat three pieces of toast.

WRITING

Objective
To practice writing numbers in a counting book about daily events.

Materials
- paper
- markers and crayons
- stapler
- construction paper
- scissors
- glue

Critical Thinking
- What are some ways we use numbers every day?
- How many things can you think of that you do 3 times a day? 2 times?

NUMBERS ALL AROUND

Math

Objective

To practice counting skills and number recognition.

Materials

- rope
- clothespins
- marker
- materials that can be hung on the rope (leaves, papers, socks)

Critical Thinking

- What other ways can you group hanging items on a line?
- How else could you make a counting tool?

Let's Make a Number Line

Can you find the right number of things to hang on the line?

 1 String a rope across the math area at a level children can reach. Use the marker to write numbers from 1 to 10 on the clothespins. Hang the clothespins on the line in a random order.

 2 Invite children to arrange the clothespins in order.

 3 Ask children to find the appropriate number of objects to hang from each pin. They can search inside and outside and even bring objects from home.

 4 Count the items on the line as a group activity.

A Different Measure

How can you measure without a ruler?

1

Look around the room for things to measure. Some things to try include chairs, tables, and rugs.

2

Let children start measuring with their hands or feet. Challenge them to figure out how many feet (or steps) long the room is or how many hands it takes to cross the table.

3

Now try measuring with small objects. Ask children to find out how many paper clips long a pencil is, how many beans wide a book is, how many pencils high a chair is, how many pennies long a shoe is, or how many crayons long a block is. Record their results.

4

Encourage children to find other things to measure. They might want to look outside on the playground or even at home. Children can also find other items to measure with.

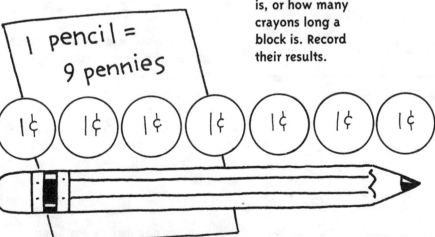

Objective

To practice measuring skills by using small objects instead of rulers.

Materials
- small objects (paper clips, pennies, beans, and so on)
- paper
- pencils

Critical Thinking
- When two children measure something with their hands or feet, are they always going to get the same answer?
- Does the size of your measuring tool affect the answer you get?

WRITING

Objective
To make signs for practical use in the classroom.

Materials
- chart paper
- paper
- markers and crayons

Critical Thinking
- Where would it be helpful to have signs with numbers outside the classroom?
- Where can you find numbers at home?

Math

Helpful Numbers
Create signs using numbers.

As a group, talk about how numbers are like a language. Ask children how words communicate information and compare this to the way in which numbers convey information.

Make a list of things that numbers tell us. Possibilities include how much, how far, how heavy, how tall, and even what time it is.

Let children examine different centers to find places where numbers are needed to communicate information. Numbers can tell how many children may be in a certain center at a time, how many cups are needed for juice, how many hats are in the dramatic-play center, or how many blocks are on certain shelves in the block center.

Invite children to make signs using numbers and post them in the room.

Paper Plate Clocks

What time is it?

1

Help children cut clock hands out of posterboard or construction paper. Use paper plates as clock faces.

2

Invite children to decorate their clock faces in an unusual way. Some children might make a clock that looks like a human face, an animal face, or a monster face. Others might want to decorate their clock as a wheel, a pie, or even a basketball.

3

Help children write numbers around the outside of the clocks. Use brass fasteners to attach clock hands to the middle of the plate.

4

As a group, figure out useful places where the clocks could be put up in the room. Clocks might show what time children arrive and leave, recess, lunchtime, and snacktime.

Objective

To reinforce number knowledge and concept of time by making and using clocks.

Materials

- paper plates
- posterboard or construction paper
- scissors
- markers and crayons
- brass fasteners

Critical Thinking

- Could you have a square clock? How about a triangle clock?
- If you don't have a clock, what other clues can you use to tell the time?

Objective

To practice pattern concepts by making place mats.

Materials

- construction paper
- scissors
- glue
- clear contact paper

Critical Thinking

- What are some other materials you can use for making patterns?
- What makes some patterns harder to find than others?

Pattern Place Mats

Make patterns you can eat off of.

Prepare this activity by cutting shapes in a variety of colors and sizes out of construction paper. Invite children to help.

Ask children to sort shapes by color and size. Place each set (small blue triangles, large red circles) in a separate bowl.

Invite children to use shapes to make pattern place mats. Let children glue construction paper pieces onto sheets of paper to make a pattern. Some children might want to use more than one pattern in the same place mat.

Cover the place mats with clear contact paper (or laminate). During lunch or snack, children can look for patterns. The place mats can also be used in the dramatic-play area.

Patterns, Patterns, Everywhere

Search for patterns all around you.

 1

Gather sets of natural and human-made objects with patterns. Pictures can be used as well. Place objects in the science center for children to explore.

 2

Encourage children to compare these objects to discover similarities and differences. Ask children to find the patterns in the objects.

3

Invite children to choose a pattern to reproduce with crayons or markers. As a group, talk about the patterns children have drawn. Make a list of other things with patterns (in nature or made by people) that children have seen.

4

To extend the activity, take a walk outside and look for patterns. Ask children to compare human-made and natural patterns and to describe their differences.

Objective

To observe and compare patterns in nature and in human-made objects.

Materials

- patterned human-made objects (cloth, wallpaper, dishes, clothing)
- patterned natural objects (leaves, flowers, shells)
- paper
- markers and crayons
- chart paper

Critical Thinking

- Why do you think patterns in nature are different from patterns in objects made by people?

Math

LANGUAGE

Objective

To use language to communicate a pattern.

Materials
- string or yarn
- colored beads (plastic or wooden)

Critical Thinking
- How else can you communicate a pattern to a friend?
- Were your strings the same or different? How do you think that happened?

Math

String Along Like Me

Can you make identical bead patterns?

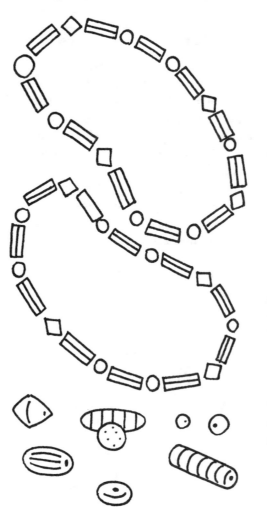

 Create two identical sets of beads.

 Invite two children to sit back to back. Give each child an identical set of beads to string. One child begins by saying "I am putting on a red bead now." The other child follows his directions. Children can also take turns choosing beads and giving directions.

 Let children continue stringing beads until the string is finished. Then they can compare strings to see whether the patterns match.

 For an added challenge, children can try to string beads of identical color, shape, and even size. For example, "I am stringing a small round red bead."

Copycat
Listen carefully to the beat.

1

Invite children to sit in a circle for a special music time. Begin by clapping or tapping a steady beat.

2

Once children can follow a steady beat, clap or tap a simple pattern for them to follow. As children become accustomed to following you, increase the length and complexity of patterns. You can also vary the tempo, or speed, of the patterns.

3

Allow children to tap out rhythms of their own for their friends to follow.

4

As a variation, play music with a strong beat and invite children to tap or clap along. Some types of Irish and African music work well for this.

MUSIC

Objective
To follow rhythmic patterns.

Materials
• rhythm sticks (or any sticks that can be used for tapping)

Critical Thinking
• Can counting help you keep track of the rhythm?
• Does the same rhythm sound different when it is made with different instruments?

PATTERNS

Math

Objective

To sort and classify a variety of objects by size.

Materials

- 2 cardboard boxes, 1 large and 1 small
- large and small objects for sorting
- markers and crayons
- construction paper
- scissors
- glue

Critical Thinking

- How did you decide whether something should go into the big box or the little box?
- What would be too big or too little for the game?

Big and Little Game

What is big and what is little?

1

Collect a variety of large and small objects. Possibilities include toy cars, stuffed animals, counters, unit blocks, shoes, socks, plastic animals, crayons, sand toys, shells, and leaves.

2

Invite children to use markers, crayons, and construction paper to decorate a large and small box for a game. Children can also help write "big" and "little" on the boxes.

3

Let children play the Big and Little Game. They can put the large objects in the big box and small objects in the little box.

4

As a challenge, ask children to sort objects based on their "real" size. For example, a plastic elephant would go into the big box and a toy mouse would go into the little box.

Move Like This

Copy a friend's actions on a different scale.

1

Let children form pairs. Ask them to choose one to be the leader and one to be the follower.

2

Invite the leaders to make big movements. They can use their arms, legs, hands, feet, and even heads. Encourage the followers to copy the movements but make them small. Then have the leaders make little movements. This time the followers should copy the movements but make them big.

3

Ask the pairs to switch roles.

4

Challenge children to act out a familiar story such as *The Three Little Pigs*, using big and little movements.

MOVEMENT

Objective
To reinforce concepts of "big" and "little" through movement.

Materials
• none

Critical Thinking
• Was it easier to make big movements little or little movements big?
• What would happen if you tried to copy the movements of a very little animal? A very big animal?

Math

Objective

To use size words to introduce the concept of "superlatives."

Materials

- similar objects of different sizes (bowls, plates, feathers, spoons, blocks)
- chart paper
- markers and crayons
- paper

Critical Thinking

- What other size words can you use to compare things?
- What are other words for *big*? What are other words for *little*?

Math

The Biggest One of All
Have fun comparing things by size.

 1

As a group, discuss the concept of "superlatives." You could begin with an example like "This bear is big. This bear is bigger. And this bear is the biggest one of all." Include examples of big and little objects.

 2

Place similar objects of different sizes on the table. Ask children to arrange objects by size. They can also label them "big, bigger, biggest" or "little, littler, littlest."

 3

Let children choose an object and illustrate it in three different sizes. Then let them write or dictate size labels for their drawings.

 4

As an extension, read *The Three Bears* and invite children to label objects in the book by size.

Prints and Rubbings

Make art with the help of big and small objects.

1 Collect various objects for making prints and rubbings. Include objects of all different sizes.

2 For rubbings, let children place paper over flat objects. Encourage them to choose objects of different sizes. Show them how to use the side of a crayon to make a rubbing.

3 Children can write or dictate size labels for their rubbings: small, medium, and big.

4 For prints, children can dip objects (sponges, cookie cutters, toy cars) into paint and make prints on construction paper or butcher paper. When finished, children can label their prints according to the size of the objects used to make them.

Objective

To explore concepts of "big" and "small" through art.

Materials

- objects for making rubbings (leaves, coins, paper clips, keys)
- objects for making prints (cotton swabs, cookie cutters, sponges)
- crayons
- paint
- white paper, construction paper, butcher paper

Critical Thinking

- Can you always tell which object made which print?

Math

Objective

To reinforce basic concepts of quantity.

Materials

- things that come in singles (hats, sweaters, scarves, and so on)
- things that come in pairs (gloves, socks, shoes, and so on)
- pillowcase or bag

Critical Thinking

- What other number groupings do objects come in?
- Can you think of some other number words?

Math

Ones and Twos

Find things that come in singles and pairs.

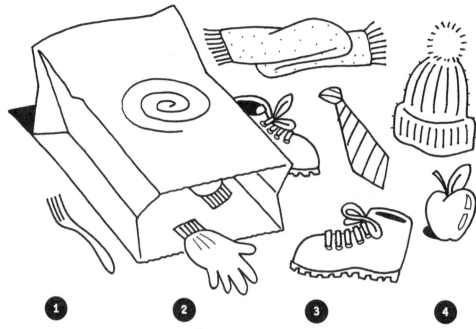

1 As a group, talk about number words. Things that are by themselves are called singles, and things that come in twos are called pairs.

2 Find things on your body that come in singles, like heads, noses, and mouths, and in pairs, like feet, arms, and hands.

3 Gather objects that come in singles and pairs. For some things, pictures can also be used. Place items in a pillowcase or "mystery bag."

4 Invite children to pull objects out of the bag and sort them into singles and pairs. Count to find out whether there were more singles or more pairs.

Three Stories of 3
Triple the fun!

As a group, read stories featuring the number 3. Make these books available for children to read on their own.

If possible, move a flannel board and characters into the math area for children to use in telling the stories. Flannel board characters can also be made by copying and coloring pages from the book. Cut out and laminate the pieces, and attach Velcro to the back.

Encourage children to create their own stories that include the number 3. Some children might want to use counters, felt pieces, or toy animals to create their stories.

Have a special story time when children can tell the "number 3" stories they have created.

LANGUAGE

Objective
To emphasize concepts of "three" using familiar stories.

Materials
- stories featuring the number 3 (*The Three Bears, Three Billy Goats Gruff,* and *The Three Little Pigs*)
- flannel board and characters (if possible)
- counters
- felt pieces
- toy animals

Critical Thinking
- Why do you think the number 3 is popular in stories?

Math

Objective

To practice counting using a variety of songs.

Materials

• none

Critical Thinking

• Can you find things to count in other songs?
• Can you make up a number dance?

Math

Counting Songs

Sing along to practice numbers.

1 Gather children for a special "Numbers" circle time.

2 Sing a song involving numbers. "This Old Man" is a good one to start with: *This old man, he played one. He played knick knack on my thumb, with a knick knack paddy whack, give a dog a bone. This old man came rolling home.* Repeat, using the following numbers and rhymes: *Two. . . shoe, Three. . . knee, Four. . . door, Five. . . hive.*

3 Let children act out the verses as you sing them. For an added twist, children can make up new verses and act them out.

4 Children might want to sing other songs about numbers. Some songs to try include "Five Little Ducks (Went Out One Day)," "Ten in a Bed," "Five Little Monkeys (Jumping on the Bed)," "Three Blind Mice," "The Ants Go Marching," and "Three Little Monkeys (Swinging in the Tree)."

This old man, he played one, he played

Simon Says "Count!"

Try a new spin on some familiar games.

1

Play a counting version of "Simon Says." Begin with yourself as the leader. Children do what the leader says, but only if the instruction includes "Simon says."

2

Use numbers in Simon's instructions. You might include the following: "Simon says jump three times," "Simon says touch your head four times," "Tap your foot two times." After becoming familiar with the game, children can take turns being the leader.

3

Try other games as counting games, such as "Red Rover" or "Mother May I?" To play "Red Rover," use descriptions instead of names. "Red Rover, Red Rover, let blue shirts (or brown hair, or tennis shoes) come over!" Then count the number of children who have come over.

4

Challenge children to invent counting games of their own.

tap
2
times

Objective
To enhance number awareness through games.

Materials
• none

Critical Thinking
• Can you think of any games or sport in which numbers are important?
• Why do you think numbers are an important part of some games?

How Many Can Play?

Math

SCIENCE

Objective

To investigate work done by a particular kind of scientist.

Materials

• different kinds of plants and flowers
• magnifying glasses
• microscopes (if available)
• newspaper
• paper
• pencils
• markers and crayons

Critical Thinking

• What other ways can botanists find out about plants?
• What senses do you use to learn about plants?

Scientists at Work
What do botanists do?

1 Gather different kinds of plants and flowers. You might want to cut some up so that children can see different parts (petals, stems, leaves) more clearly.

2 Invite children to use magnifying glasses and microscopes to examine and compare plants. Children can also press plants between newspaper pages. Let the plants dry between the pages for a few days, and then have children observe the changes. Encourage children to record their observations.

3 Go for a nature walk to find more plants. Children can draw the plants they find. Encourage them to note as many details as possible. Other plants can be gathered for further observation in the classroom.

4 As an extension, visit the library for books on plants. Have a group discussion about what you have learned in your botany studies.

Science Time Line

Observe carefully how things change.

day 1   day 5

1 Put out a slice each of bread, peach, and strawberry for 24 hours. Let children observe the food throughout the day, and have them record their observations with drawings.

2 On day 2, pour two teaspoons of water on the bread. Place the bread, peach, and strawberry in individual resealable bags. Invite each child to choose a food to observe. If possible, place bags in a sunny spot.

3 Every day (or every two days), let children observe the changes in the food. Encourage them to record their observations with drawings and words. Children can use a separate page for each day of observation.

4 After one week, join the pages together to make a time line that shows the changes in the food. You might also laminate some of the drawings to make cards and allow children to put them in order.

Objective
To record change on a time line.

Materials
- bread, peach, strawberry
- water
- resealable plastic bag
- paper
- markers and crayons

Critical Thinking
- What other ways can you record change?
- Where do you think the mold on the bread (or fruit) came from?

Scientists
Pamela Chanko • Samantha Berger
SCHOLASTIC

COOKING

Objective

To practice science skills through baking bread.

Materials

- large bowl, spoon, towel, baking sheet, knife, oven
- ruler
- paper
- pencils
- chart paper
- markers
- ingredients

Critical Thinking

- Who else uses science skills in their work?
- What are some other things you do at school that use science skills?

Be a Cooking Scientist
What kind of science do chefs do?

 1

Let children help you mix sugar, salt, yeast, and water in a bowl. Stir in 5 cups flour. Knead the dough on a floured surface until smooth and elastic. Put it in a greased bowl. Turn once.

 2

Allow children to examine the uncooked dough with as many senses as possible. Have them record how it looks, smells, feels, and tastes. Children can also use rulers to measure its height.

 3

Cover dough with a damp towel and set it aside to rise. After 60–90 minutes, children can examine the dough again. Let children record the new height, along with any other changes they observe. Shape dough into four loaves, slash the crusts, and brush with beaten egg.

 4

Bake dough in the oven for 15 minutes at 450 degrees. Reduce heat to 350 degrees, and bake for another 30 minutes. When the bread has finished baking, record changes in appearance, temperature, smell, taste, texture, and height. Finally, eat and enjoy!

Ingredients

2 tablespoons sugar
1 tablespoon salt
1 package dry yeast
$2\frac{1}{2}$ cups warm water
6 cups flour
1 egg

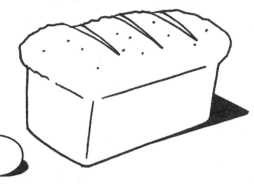

Sounds of Science

How can you make music?

Let children help you pour water into the glasses (leaving one empty) so that each glass has a different amount of water.

Children can use sticks to tap the glasses and note the sounds they make. Children might want to order the glasses based on sound, from lowest to highest. They also might want to try using the glasses to tap out a tune.

Children can try tapping the glasses with a metal spoon or find other surfaces to tap. Encourage children to compare sounds made by hollow and solid objects. They can also compare sounds made by tapping different materials, such as wood, metal, glass, and plastic.

After they listen to different sounds, challenge children to identify sounds with their eyes closed (or blindfolded).

MUSIC

Objective
To compare sounds made by glasses filled with different levels of water.

Materials
- several glasses of the same size
- pitcher
- water
- wooden sticks
- spoons

Critical Thinking
- How are sounds produced by human-made objects similar to and different from sounds in nature?
- How is your voice like an instrument?

Science

Objective

To use science skills to hunt for items outdoors.

Materials

- paper
- pencils
- crayons and markers
- index cards

Critical Thinking

- What made some things on the lists harder to find than others?
- When do you use science skills at home?

Science Scavenger Hunt

Be a scientist outdoors.

1 In advance, prepare lists of items for children to hunt for. Some lists might include specific items to be collected (twigs, leaves, seeds, rocks, and feathers). Other lists might be based on textures (items that are soft, fuzzy, bumpy, hard, scratchy) or shapes (items that are circular, triangular, heart-shaped, star-shaped).

2 For a challenge, give children lists of items that require them to use comparison skills. Possibilities include two flowers that have different numbers of petals, two leaves that are the same shape but different sizes, and three flat rocks that are different colors.

3 You might also make a list of things that require careful observation skills, such as watching a bird feeding its baby, ants carrying food, or leaves blowing in the wind. Encourage children to record their observations of these events.

4 As a group, discuss the items that children found and the observations they made. Ask children which science skills they used (comparing, observing, watching, listening, recording) on their hunts.

4 petals

6 petals

big leaf

small leaf

Science Journals

Watch carefully as a puddle evaporates.

 1

Prepare science journals by stapling paper together. Children might want to decorate the covers with markers or crayons.

 2

Use observation skills outdoors. Find a puddle that has formed, or create one on the playground. Have children observe the puddle and record their observations in their science journals.

 3

Let children watch the puddle as it evaporates. They can note how long it takes to evaporate, what happened when the sky was sunny or cloudy, and what was left behind after the puddle evaporated. Children can use pictures or words (or both) to record their observations.

4

Try to find other things to observe outdoors. Children can use their journals to record observations of the growth of a weed or flower, leaves budding from a twig, a bird building a nest, or ants building an anthill.

WRITING

Objective
To practice observation and recording skills by creating a journal.

Materials
- paper
- stapler
- markers and crayons
- pencils
- chart paper

Critical Thinking
- Did everyone make the same observations about the same event, or did some notice different things?
- What other ways can you record what you see?

Science Outside
Susan Canizares
Betsey Chessen

Science

Objective

To make art with materials collected on a nature walk.

Materials

- masking tape
- plastic bags
- clear contact paper
- crayons
- paper
- glue
- glitter
- paint

Critical Thinking

- Did some things you collected stick to the masking tape better than others?
- Does your collection give you any clues about what season it is?

Natural Art

Have you ever seen jewelry like this?

Help children use masking tape to make a bracelet by forming a loop, sticky side out.

Go for a nature walk and let children create jewelry as they go. Let them attach objects, such as leaves, grass, flowers, and twigs, to the masking tape. They can put additional items in a plastic bag. Remind children to be careful not to pick up dangerous objects such as broken glass.

After returning to the classroom, invite children to use other items to make art. Children can make a collage on contact paper. They can also use crayons and paper to make leaf rubbings.

As an extension, make "nature creatures." Encourage children to make animals out of leaves, twigs, rocks, and grass. They can even add paint and glitter.

Sound Graph

What do you hear when you take a silent walk?

1

As a group, choose a walking path that will include many different sounds. If possible, include streets or crowded areas as well as quieter places like parks or woods.

2

Walk along the path in silence. Have children write down all the sounds they hear. Encourage them to stop frequently and close their eyes so they can listen more closely to all the sounds around them.

3

After returning to the classroom, help children combine their individual lists into a class list.

4

Make a bar graph of the sounds you heard on the walk. Find out if children were surprised by any sounds they heard and whether all children heard (or noticed) the same sounds.

bzzzz

chirp

beep!

Objective

To graph sounds heard on a walk.

Materials
- clipboards
- pencils
- paper
- marker
- chart paper

Critical Thinking
- How could you tell what was making a particular sound?
- Did you hear more natural sounds or human-made sounds? Why?

Science Outside
Susan Canizares
Betsey Chessen
SCHOLASTIC

Objective

To become familiar with funnels by using them in an experiment.

Materials

- soil samples
- funnels
- cloth
- rubber bands
- clear jars
- measuring cups
- water
- pencils
- paper

Critical Thinking

- What are some other tools scientists might use?
- Are there some tools that work better inside than outside?

Experiment With Tools

Try out tools scientists use.

1 Children can collect soil samples from home, the playground, or nearby areas. Try to include samples of sandy and clay soils. Keep the different kinds of soil separate.

2 Fasten a piece of cloth over the small end of the funnels and place each funnel over a jar. Let children help you measure equal amounts of each kind of soil and pour the soil into the funnels.

3 Children can measure water into each funnel (an amount approximately equal to the soil in each funnel). Let children pour the water into the funnels and observe it as it percolates through the soil.

4 Then help children measure how much water collects in each jar. Next, children can figure out and record how much water each kind of soil can hold.

Super Science

Turn your dramatic-play area into a scientists' lab.

1

Add science tools to the dramatic-play area. Include props such as lab coats, if possible.

2

Invite children to role-play different science scenarios. They could pretend to cure a strange disease, or even the common cold. Some children might want to invent a new computer or robot, or a machine to cook dinner or pack lunches. Others might want to explore what the surfaces of objects look like close up.

3

If possible, do real "chemistry" experiments by exploring and mixing colored water, baking soda, cornstarch, and other materials.

4

Let children record their experiments and discoveries on paper. They can also combine their findings into a "super science" notebook.

Objective
To use science tools in role-playing.

Materials
- science tools (funnels, rulers, magnifying glasses, tweezers, measuring cups, paper, and pencils)
- lab coats (or white shirts)
- microscope (if available)

Critical Thinking
- If you could do any kind of experiment, what would you like to find out?

Science

Objective

To use a science tool to create art.

Materials

- eyedroppers
- bowls
- water
- food coloring
- tempera paint
- paper towels
- fabric scraps
- coffee filters
- tissue paper
- paper

Critical Thinking

- Which surfaces were better for eyedropper art?
- What other objects can you paint with?

Eyedropper Art

What can you do with drips and drops?

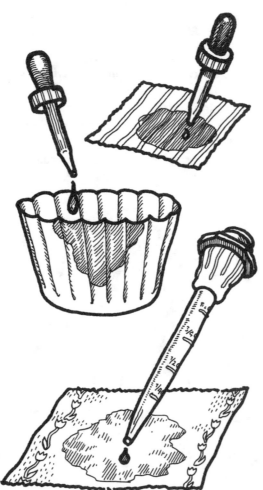

 1

Mix a few drops of food coloring in water. Tempera paint can also be used.

 2

Let children choose a material (paper towels, paper, coffee filters, or tissue paper) to paint on. They can use eyedroppers instead of paintbrushes to make pictures. Ask children to find out what happens when they use a lot of liquid or just a little. What happens when they put one color on top of another?

 3

Encourage children to compare different surfaces and how they absorb the color (or liquid). They can also experiment with different color patterns.

 4

Have children try making art with other science tools. Let them invent new art uses for funnels, rulers, and magnifying glasses.

Stethoscope Fun

Listen to your heart.

Let children listen to their heartbeats with a stethoscope. Then show children how to feel their heartbeats by putting their fingers on the side of their windpipes.

Let children observe their heartbeats after running, jumping up and down, lying down for 10 minutes, or splashing cold water on their faces. Children can use stethoscopes or their own hands to monitor their heartbeats.

Encourage children to compare how long it takes for their heart rate to go back down (to a resting pace) after exercising for different lengths of time.

As a group, discuss what makes your heart beat faster or slower. List children's observations on chart paper, and add to the list as children discover additional activities that make their heart rates speed up and slow down.

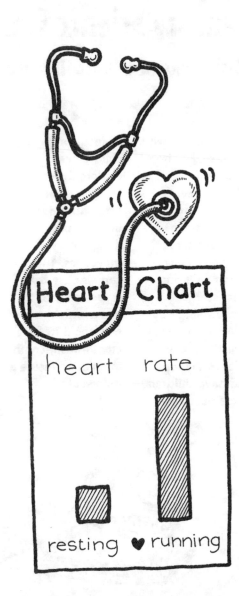

MOVEMENT

Objective
To use a stethoscope to observe heartbeats.

Materials
- stethoscope
- chart paper
- marker
- area for movement

Critical Thinking
- What else changes when your heart beats faster?
- Where else can you feel your heartbeat?

SCIENCE TOOLS

Susan Canizares • Betsey Chessen
SCHOLASTIC

Science

Objective

To practice making observations with various senses.

Materials

- cotton balls
- film canisters
- various scents
- objects to make different sounds
- textured materials
- household items
- pillowcase
- colored cellophane or tissue paper
- kaleidoscope

Critical Thinking

- What do you notice with your eyes closed that you might miss with your eyes open?

Sensory Science Center

Can you see/smell/touch/hear it?

1

To experiment with smell, soak cotton balls with different scents (peppermint, vanilla, lemon) or oils (suntan oil, baby oil). Place cotton balls and other scents (cinnamon, baby powder) in film canisters. Poke holes in the top and have children guess the smells.

2

To focus on touch, children can explore different textures such as sandpaper, fur, netting, play dough, or pinecones. They can also use their sense of touch to guess which household items (toothbrush, comb) are hidden inside a pillowcase.

3

For sight, let children observe the colors in a kaleidoscope or explore what happens when they layer different colors of cellophane or tissue paper.

4

For hearing, place different objects in film canisters, such as bells, rice, beans, or confetti. Have children shake the canisters and guess the contents, based on what they hear.

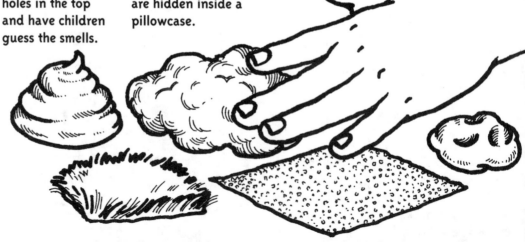

Shiny Penny

Does it smell like vinegar?

 1

As a group, look at the old pennies. Set out salt, vinegar, and water, and ask children to predict what combination will clean the penny. Record their predictions.

 2

Children can try different combinations such as salt and water, vinegar and water, and so on. (The combination of vinegar and salt will clean the pennies!)

 3

Encourage children to try the solution they think will clean by rubbing it on the penny with a cotton swab. (Pennies can also be placed directly into the solution.) Dry the pennies to check which solution worked.

 4

Compare the results with children's predictions.

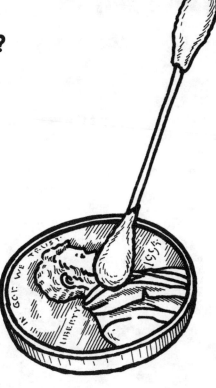

SCIENCE

Objective
To use sight and smell to explore how to clean a penny.

Materials
- old pennies
- salt
- vinegar
- water
- bowls
- cotton swabs
- paper towels
- chart paper
- marker

Critical Thinking
- What other experiments can you do to test your prediction?

Science

Objective

To make a chart about the five senses.

Materials
- pencils
- paper

Critical Thinking
- How would your life change if you could not use one of your senses?
- Why doesn't everybody have the same favorite sights, sounds, touches, smells, and tastes?

Science

The Five Senses

Take a poll about how other people use their senses.

 Help children create charts to record other people's favorite sights, smells, touches, sounds, and tastes. Write the senses across the top and children's names in a column along the left side.

 Have children interview their friends, family, and neighbors to find out their favorite things to see, smell, taste, hear, and touch.

3 Children can write or draw their results on the chart.

 As a group, talk about the responses children recorded. Find out whether any of the answers were the same. Encourage children to look for patterns, such as whether children tended to share the same favorite tastes or whether adults tended to like the same smells.

Musical Art
Draw to the beat.

As a group, talk about how you might draw a sound. Ask children to suggest what they might draw when they are listening to a favorite song.

Try it out! Play different kinds of music such as classical, blues, jazz, Celtic, African, and salsa.

Invite children to draw what they hear or what the music makes them think of. Remind children that their drawings do not have to look like a particular person or thing. Some children might even want to try drawing with their eyes closed.

Compare different drawings. Let children guess what kind of music was being played while different drawings were made.

ART

Objective
To listen carefully to music and draw what you hear.

Materials
- different kinds of recorded music
- paper
- markers and crayons

Critical Thinking
- How would you draw a smell or a taste?
- Did everyone's drawings to the same music look the same?

Objective

To investigate how objects with the same function have changed in form.

Materials

- old and new objects
- boxes labeled "Old" and "New"

Critical Thinking

- What do you think cars or clothes will look like in 100 years?
- If you could create an invention for the future, what would it be?

Old and New

How have these household objects changed?

1

Gather old and new objects, such as toys, tools, eating utensils, books, clothing, and appliances, and place them in the science center. You might ask parents to contribute items from home. Pictures can also be used for this activity.

2

Invite children to examine and compare the objects. They can look for the ways objects have changed and look for similarities among the objects.

3

Encourage children to sort objects into the "Old" and "New" boxes.

4

As a group, discuss ways in which things have changed since the old objects were made. Also discuss what has stayed the same.

Then and Now Stories

Make up an adventure about old times.

 1

As a group, look at "then and now" photos. Talk about what life was like in the "then" photos and how it was different from life in the "now" photos.

 2

Invite children to write or dictate an adventure story about life long ago. They can look at the "then" photos for ideas about the lives of characters in their stories.

 3

If children have difficulty beginning their stories, encourage them to write about what would happen if a person living now went back 100 years in time.

4

Let children illustrate their stories and share them with the group.

WRITING

Objective

To think about how things in people's daily lives have changed over time.

Materials

- photos of old and new houses, clothing, vehicles, appliances
- paper
- pencils
- crayons

Critical Thinking

- If you could live 100 years ago, now, or 100 years in the future, which would you choose? Why?
- What invention would make your life easier? More fun?

Science

LANGUAGE

Objective

To compare ourselves now with how we used to be.

Materials

- pictures of children as infants
- current pictures of children
- posterboard
- glue
- chart paper
- markers

Critical Thinking

- What can you do now that you couldn't do when you were younger?
- What would you like to be able to do when you are older?

Science

All Grown Up

How have we grown?

Ask children to bring in pictures of themselves as infants and current pictures. (Current pictures can also be taken in the classroom.)

Glue pictures of children as infants onto one posterboard and current pictures onto another. Vary the order of the pictures on each posterboard. Ask children to guess who's who by matching pictures.

Let children write their names below their pictures. They might also want to use markers to decorate the surrounding posterboard.

As a group, talk about ways children have changed since they were babies. Children can describe changes in size, abilities, interests, and even likes and dislikes. Make a list of all the changes children can think of.

Time Travel

Use props to go back in time.

Objective

To become more familiar with other time periods through role play.

Materials

- old clothes
- old kitchen utensils or household items (if possible)
- large appliance box
- utility knife
- paintbrushes
- paint

Critical Thinking

- What other ways can you find out about life before you were born?
- What person from long ago would you most like to meet?

1

Enlist children's help in collecting old props such as clothes or household items from parents and grandparents.

2

Invite children to use paint to transform a cardboard box into a time machine. They can paint the inside and outside and help cut out windows and a door.

3

Let children use the time machine to travel to other periods. Props can be used to act out life in other times. Children can role-play going to work or parties, eating meals, and playing games in different eras.

4

As an extension, visit the library or bring in books to research customs from "olden" times. Children can act out customs like a tea party in the 1920s or even a 1950s sock hop!

Objective

To practice writing and language skills by inventing story endings.

Materials

- sentence strips
- marker
- paper
- pencils
- crayons

Critical Thinking

- How would you start a story about your family? Your class?

- Were some sentences (story beginnings) harder to finish than others?

Story Starters

Can you finish these stories?

 1

Write various story beginnings on sentence strips. Some can be the beginnings to familiar stories, such as "Three bears lived in a house in the woods" or "Once upon a time, there were three little pigs." Others can be more open-ended, such as "I took a trip in a rocket ship" or "When I dove into the ocean, I saw…"

 2

Introduce the sentence strips into the writing center for children to use in creating stories. Children can copy the beginnings onto a sheet of paper and then continue the story by writing or dictating.

 3

Encourage children to illustrate their stories with crayons.

 4

Children can also try to invent several different endings for the same beginning.

Reasons to Write

What should we write about?

1

As a group, brainstorm reasons for writing. Encourage children to think of as many reasons as they can. Make a class list. As children think of new ideas, add them to the list.

2

Invite children to help you make a chart of reasons to write. The chart might include letters to family and friends, grocery lists, recipes, to-do lists, schedules, party invitations, and get-well cards or birthday cards.

3

Place the chart in the writing center, and allow children to refer to it for writing suggestions.

4

As an alternative, children can copy the reasons onto index cards. Laminate the cards and place them in an envelope for children to choose from when they need an idea for writing.

Objective

To create a reference chart for writing suggestions.

Materials
- chart paper
- marker
- posterboard
- paper
- pencils
- crayons
- index cards
- envelope

Critical Thinking
- How is writing like talking? How is it different?
- Are there some times when drawing or showing works better than writing?

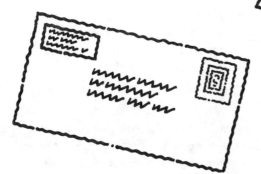

Objective

To role-play scenarios that involve writing.

Materials

- pencils
- crayons
- scissors
- magazines, newspaper flyers
- paper
- notepads
- used checkbooks
- calendar

Critical Thinking

- What other times can making lists help you?
- Do you use writing in any rooms in your home?

Shopping Day

Make a list and check it twice.

food to
buy:
apples
oranges
bread
milk

Have a shopping day in the dramatic-play center. To begin, figure out what you need to buy.

Invite children to make lists of what they need to shop for. Some children might want to check the refrigerator and cabinets and make a list of needed food. Others can look around and make lists of utensils or other household items. Others might even want to make lists of clothes they would like to buy.

Let children pretend to go shopping. They can make pretend money and cut out pictures from magazines and newspapers of items to buy and sell.

Ask children to role-play other ways to use writing in the dramatic-play center. Children can write down recipes, rules, or chores that need to be done.

Farm Plans

Make your own blueprints.

Have a class discussion about the kinds of buildings you might find on a farm. Encourage children to think about different kinds of farms—cattle ranches, wheat farms, vegetable farms, or even farms that have more than one kind of product.

Invite children to design their own farms. They can use writing to make "blueprints." Have them indicate the kinds of animals and farm equipment that go in each building and label other areas of the farms. Children can use rulers to make straight lines for buildings and fences.

Let children use blocks to build their farms according to plans they have drawn.

As a challenge, encourage children to try to follow each other's farm plan.

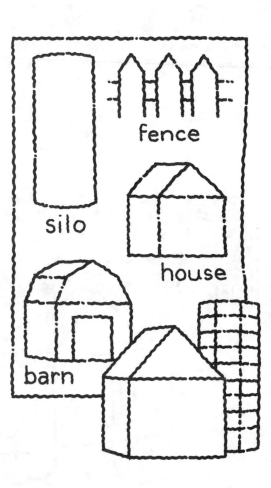

silo

fence

house

barn

BLOCKS

Objective
To use writing to plan farm buildings.

Materials
- blocks
- paper
- pencils
- rulers
- chart paper
- markers

Critical Thinking
- Did you have to change any of your plans once you started building?
- If you made an addition to your farm plans, would you describe it with words, drawings, or both? Why?

Objective

To create a wall for free-form writing.

Materials

- butcher paper
- markers and crayons

Critical Thinking

- If people wrote on a blank wall, what would it look like after a few days?
- How could you change the floor to make it into a writing surface?

Writing on the Wall

Graffiti is allowed here.

Choose a wall to be the designated writing wall. Cover it with butcher paper.

Let children write on the wall. They can write stories; messages to friends, teachers, or parents; observations; to-do list; rules; or even their own names.

Try adding "themes" to your writing wall. Children might make a calendar for the week or the month, a daily schedule, or "welcome back" greetings to a friend who has been out sick.

To extend the activity, let children decorate their writing with illustrations.

A Different Alphabet

Create your own secret code.

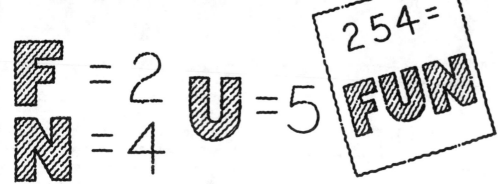

Objective

To invent an alphabet code and use it to create messages.

Materials

- examples of other (non-Roman) alphabets or writing
- paper
- pencils

Critical Thinking

- How else can you create a code?
- What clues can you use to crack a new code?

1

Bring in examples of alphabets or symbol systems used in languages other than English. Possibilities include Greek and Cyrillic (Russian) alphabets and Japanese, Chinese, and Korean characters. Let children examine different writing samples.

2

Invite children to create their own symbol systems. For instance, children might choose to assign a number to each letter (A=1, B=2, and so on). Children can help you make a chart showing the new symbol (or number) next to the matching standard symbol.

3

If this is too difficult, children can help create picture symbols to stand for whole words, as in the Chinese language. This is a good way to create rebus-type messages.

4

Every morning write a new word in code (or a word symbol) in the writing center. Children can use the chart to decode the word. Encourage them to use the code to send messages to friends as well.

MATH

MATH

Writing Places Graph

Can you write on this?

Objective

To use math skills to make a graph of writing surfaces.

Materials
• chart paper
• marker

Critical Thinking
• Are there some surfaces that you can only write on at certain times?
• Are some surfaces better than others for different kinds of messages?

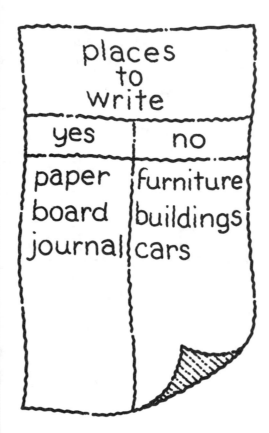

places to write

yes	no
paper	furniture
board	buildings
journal	cars

As a group, discuss writing places or surfaces. Make a list of all the things to write on. Begin with practical ideas like paper, chalkboards, posters, and cardboard boxes. Then encourage children to think of more unusual surfaces, such as sand, snow, rocks, and so on.

When the list is finished, go through it and decide which surfaces are good for writing (paper) and which are not (furniture). Write "yes" or "no" next to each surface. Ask children why the "no" surfaces are not good places to write. Make a graph of "yes" and "no" surfaces.

Discuss why there were more surfaces in the "yes" column or the "no" column.

Extend the graph by adding a "maybe" column.

Writing Tools

Can you write with it?

1

Together with children, come up with a list of writing tools. Encourage them to think of common tools, such as markers, crayons, and colored pencils, and uncommon tools, such as cotton swabs dipped in paint, twigs, and fingers (in sand, for example).

2

Let children experiment with tools from the list. They can try writing the alphabet, their names, or a note to a friend or parent.

3

Children can also use different kinds of writing surfaces, such as paper, tissue paper, cardboard, sand, and plastic.

4

Challenge children to come up with even more unusual ways of writing. Some might want to make letters out of pipe cleaners or masking tape. Others might try toothpicks or paper strips.

Objective

To expand writing skills by exploring a variety of writing tools.

Materials

- chart paper
- writing tools (markers, crayons, chalk, pencils)
- paint and brushes
- unusual writing tools (cotton swabs, twigs, chopsticks, feathers, pipe cleaners)
- writing surfaces (paper, cardboard, plastic)

Critical Thinking

- Are there any tools that people used to write with but no longer do?

Objective

To create a non-fiction book about the ocean.

Materials

- reference books about oceans, fish, and other sea creatures
- chart paper
- pencils
- crayons and markers
- paper
- stapler

Critical Thinking

- How is nonfiction different from a storybook?
- Where do you think nonfiction authors get their information?

Ocean Book

Create a nonfiction book of your own.

 Discuss the difference between fiction and non-fiction books. As a group, brainstorm questions that children have about the ocean. Collect books that can be used to answer these questions.

 Let small groups of children each choose a question to research. Children can use classroom books to search for answers, go to the library, or even ask adults (parents, teachers, scientists).

 Have children write or dictate pages with answers to the questions they chose. Some children might prefer to create pages showing different kinds of fish and ocean creatures. When finished, staple the pages together to create a book.

 Place the book in the book center to read and use as a reference. Children might also create books on other topics such as dinosaurs, bugs, or flowers.

Oceans have water. Fish live there.

A Literary Slumber Party

Use a flashlight to read under the blankets.

Have a class slumber (or pajama) party. Invite children to bring their favorite books from home. Some children might want to visit the school library to look for books to bring.

Use blankets, chairs, tables, and other classroom furniture to set up a tent (or tents) in your dramatic-play area. Put flashlights inside the tents.

Children might want to bring in their pajamas and stuffed toys from home. Hold the slumber party inside the tents. Turn out the lights and let children use flashlights to read the books they have brought.

You might include other slumber party activities, such as popping popcorn or telling ghost stories.

DRAMATIC PLAY

Objective
To read books in an unusual context.

Materials
- flashlights
- blankets
- chairs
- tables
- books
- paper
- crayons and markers
- tape

Critical Thinking
- What are other unusual places to read books?
- What is your favorite place to read?

ALL KINDS OF BOOKS

Writing

Objective

To find letters to use in an alphabet book.

Materials

- magazines
- newspapers
- paper
- scissors
- glue
- crayons and markers
- stapler

Critical Thinking

- What other types of books can you make from newspapers and magazines?
- How could you teach younger children their ABC's?

ABC Book

Hunt for the letters.

Have children search magazines and newspapers for examples of letters. Encourage them to find a variety of fonts. They can also look for uppercase and lowercase letters.

Let children cut out the letters and glue each letter of the alphabet onto a separate page.

3

Continue by letting children search for pictures of things that begin with each letter (apple, banana, and so on). Invite children to cut out pictures and glue them onto the appropriate pages. Some children might also want to draw pictures of objects that begin with certain letters.

Staple the pages together, and enjoy reading the book as a group.

The Very Hungry Caterpillar Salad

Use storybooks for cooking ideas.

1

Read *The Very Hungry Caterpillar* as a group. Ask children what they would need to make a salad based on the book.

2

Let children help you make a fruit salad. Count out the numbers of different kinds of fruit the caterpillar ate (1 apple, 2 pears, 3 plums). Children can decorate the outside of the bowl with leaves (washed, of course).

3

After enjoying the salad, let children write down and illustrate the recipe. They can show how many apples, oranges, and so on to use and list the steps for making the salad (washing the fruit, cutting it up, mixing the salad).

4

Have children think of other recipes based on favorite stories. Some possibilities include jam sandwiches (*Bread and Jam for Frances*) and porridge (*The Three Bears, Goodnight Moon*). Add these recipes to the book.

Hungry Caterpillar Salad
1 apple
2 pears
3 plums

Objective
To start a class recipe book based on stories

Materials
- copy of *The Very Hungry Caterpillar*
- apples, pears, plum strawberries, orang
- leaves
- bowl
- cutting board and k
- crayons and marke
- paper

Critical Thinking
- What else could you cook that the very hungry caterpillar might enjoy?
- Do people and animals eat the same foods?

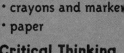

ALL KINDS OF BOOKS

Writing

Objective

To create informational signs for the classroom.

Materials

- paper
- markers and crayons
- tape

Critical Thinking

- What kinds of "how to" signs would help a visitor in your home? In the grocery store?
- Where would a sign with more than two languages on it be helpful?

"How to" Signs

What would a visitor from Mars need to know?

1

As a group, imagine what would happen if a visitor from outer space came to your school. Discuss how you would explain to this visitor how things are done in your classroom.

2

Invite children to walk around the room, and perhaps the playground, to identify where informational signs might be helpful.

3

Small groups of children can create "how to" signs to help the visitor. Children might create signs about how to pass out snacks, how to put away blocks, how to do show-and-tell, how to use the math center, or even how to swing on the swings. Encourage children to use a combination of letters and symbols.

4

Let children help you put up the signs. Invite children from other classes to test them to see if they can understand them.

Signs Without Words

Pictures only.

1
Collect examples of signs without words for children to examine. Possibilities include walk (person walking) and stop (hand) signals, a traffic light, a road sign with a wavy line (curves ahead), or a U-turn sign.

2
Invite children to create wordless signs of their own. They can use markers and crayons or cut out pictures from magazines to use in their signs.

3
Children can display their signs around the room. Encourage children to guess what the signs mean.

4
Let children add words to their signs. Ask them whether words make the signs clearer or more confusing.

Objective
To communicate through signs without using words.

Materials
- paper
- markers and crayons
- magazines
- scissors
- glue

Critical Thinking
- Why do you think sign makers sometimes use pictures?
- What kinds of signs should use only words?

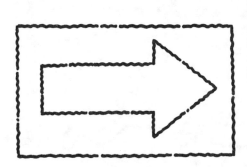

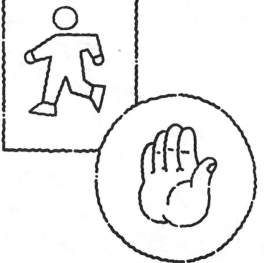

Writing

Objective

To use writing to create an advertisement sign.

Materials

- paper
- pencils
- markers and crayons
- magazines

Critical Thinking

- How are advertisements different from informational signs?
- Can you think of any words that are often used in advertisements? What do these words have in common?

Design Your Own Ad
Make a mini-billboard.

 Many signs are advertisements. As a group, discuss advertisements that children have seen, the products they are for, and what ads try to do. Let children look through magazines for ads, and have them explain what the ads are trying to sell.

 Look around the school and neighborhood for signs that are used as advertisements.

 Invite children to choose (or invent) a product and create an ad to sell it. Ads could be for a favorite toy, game, snack, or even a place to visit.

 Encourage children to review one another's ads. Children can discuss whether the ads would make them want to buy the product. As an extension, some children might even want to create an ad for TV and act it out with friends.

Eat Dino Crunch

International "No" Signs

Some rules are universal.

(1)
Find examples of international "no" signs (a picture inside a circle with a slash through it). Explain how this symbol always means that something is not allowed. For example, a car inside a circle with a slash through it means "no cars allowed."

(2)
Cut circles out of paper or posterboard. Invite children to use them to create signs of their own. Ask them to think about what their signs will forbid and where the signs will be placed. Children can draw pictures, cut out pictures from magazines, or cut figures from construction paper. They can finish by gluing a slash across the circle.

(3)
Have a special show-and-tell, and let children guess one another's signs. Children can explain what their signs forbid and where their signs might be found.

(4)
Encourage children to look for other examples of international "no" signs in books, magazines, and around town.

Objective
To design international symbol signs.

Materials
- paper or posterboard
- scissors
- pencils
- crayons and markers
- magazines
- construction paper
- glue

Critical Thinking
- Why are there some places where cars, pets, or food are not allowed?

Writing

Objective

To create a fictional animal.

Materials
- paper
- pencils
- markers and crayons

Critical Thinking
- How is the animal you created different from a real animal (or a pet)?
- If your character came to life for a day, how do you think your day would change?

Animal Character

Make a "Huggly" of your own.

Invite each child to invent a fictional animal character. Let children draw their characters.

Have children create a "biography" about themselves and their animals. Questions to think about include what they like to eat, what they like to do, where they live, what they like to play, and what they do together.

Encourage children to draw pictures to illustrate their biographies. They can write descriptions underneath the pictures.

Extend the activity by having children illustrate the differences between their characters and themselves.

A Letter to Tedd

Send a note to the author.

Objective
To write a class letter to an author.

Materials
• chart paper
• paper
• pencils
• crayons and markers

Critical Thinking
• If you could write a letter to Huggly, what would you tell him?
• What adventure with Huggly would you like to write about?

1

As a class, brainstorm things children would like to tell Tedd Arnold. Record children's ideas on chart paper.

2

Help children decide what messages to include in the letter. Some children can help write the letter, and others might illustrate it.

3

Send the letter to: Tedd Arnold P.O. Box 4363 Elmira, NY 14904. (Teachers: Please send only one letter per class. Do not display or distribute this address.)

4

Be sure to include a self-addressed, stamped envelope. Check your mailbox for a response from Tedd!

Objective

To involve children more deeply in stories through role play.

Materials
• favorite books
• chart paper
• markers

Critical Thinking
• If you could meet the creator of any character, who would it be?
• What would you ask your favorite author or illustrator?

Favorite Character Day
Who's your favorite story character?

1

Invite children to come to school as their favorite characters from storybooks. To prepare, write a note to parents about the special day.

2

On Story Character Day, have children guess what characters their friends have come as. Children can give clues by role-playing things their characters do. For example, Goldilocks could try out some chairs and Pooh could search for honey!

3

Encourage children to create new stories that involve characters from different books. Alice in Wonderland could go to Eeyore's birthday party. Children can role-play these scenarios in the dramatic-play center.

4

Place favorite storybooks in the dramatic-play center for children to use in creating additional scenarios.

Make Your Own Monster

Create creatures out of clay.

Objective

To sculpt new characters from clay.

Materials
- clay
- pipe cleaners
- felt
- googly eyes
- various collage materials

Critical Thinking
- Are all monsters scary?
- What other creatures can you make out of clay?

1

Invite children to dream up their own monsters. They can use clay to sculpt their monsters. If possible, let them use different-colored clay.

2

Add other materials to the monsters. Possibilities include pipe cleaners for limbs or antennae, googly eyes, felt for skin or clothes, and other collage materials.

3

Encourage children to describe their monsters to their friends. They can explain their monsters' likes and dislikes and what the monsters do when children have gone home for the day.

4

After the monsters have dried, have children bring them to a Monster Party.

INDEX

INDEX